NEW DIRECTIONS
FOR TEACHING AND
LEARNING

Number 4 • 1980

NEW DIRECTIONS FOR TEACHING AND LEARNING

A Quarterly Sourcebook
Kenneth E. Eble and John F. Noonan, Editors-in-Chief

Number 4, 1980

Learning About Teaching

John F. Noonan
Editor

Jossey-Bass Inc., Publishers
San Francisco • Washington • London

LEARNING ABOUT TEACHING
New Directions for Teaching and Learning
Number 4, 1980
   John F. Noonan, Editor

Copyright © 1980 by Jossey-Bass Inc., Publishers
and
Jossey-Bass Limited

New Directions for Teaching and Learning is published quarterly
by Jossey-Bass Inc., Publishers. Subscriptions are available
at the regular rate for institutions, libraries, and agencies
of $30 for one year. Individuals may subscribe at the special
professional rate of $18 for one year.

Correspondence:
Subscriptions, single-issue orders, change of address notices,
undelivered copies, and other correspondence should be sent to
New Directions Subscriptions, Jossey-Bass Inc., Publishers,
433 California Street, San Francisco, California 94104.

Editorial correspondence should be sent to the Editors-in-Chief,
Kenneth E. Eble or John F. Noonan, Center for Improving
Teaching Effectiveness, Virginia Commonwealth University,
Richmond, Virginia 23284.

Library of Congress Catalogue Card Number LC 80-80837
International Standard Serial Number ISSN 0271-0633
International Standard Book Number ISBN 87589-865-3

Cover design by Willi Baum
Manufactured in the United States of America

Contents

Editor's Notes

Most colleges do not have an Office of Instructional Development on which faculty can call when they want to improve their teaching techniques. And, given the economic picture, such programs are not likely to emerge on many more campuses. Suppose you are in a college that has no acknowledged experts in college pedagogy and you want to find ways to enrich your own teaching. What can you do? This volume presents ten alternatives.

To begin with, as Richard Jones shows in his chapter, "Letters of Reflection," you can replace the one- or two-sentence evaluative comment that you write at the end of a student's paper with a more personally constructed appraisal of the work, a change that will almost certainly cause you to learn more from evaluation than you thought you could. Or, like Annette Woodlief, you might keep a written record of your experiences teaching a particular course, hoping to identify through such regular recording some of your less obvious assumptions about learning. It is a way of "Including Ourselves in Our Own Courses."

A lot has been written about the value of systematic observation of teaching, but most of us are not well enough acquainted with such systems to use them, or we may even be wary of them. So, in "One-to-One Faculty Development," it is refreshing to read Peter Elbow's unapologetically unsystematic notions of visiting a colleague's classes. Have you ever wondered what happens to a teacher who tries to change altogether her approach to the classroom? Judith Newcombe kept notes along the way and chronicles her transition in "The Impacts of Change."

Even though our own college and graduate school days are far behind, it is still possible to learn from our old professors, as Thomas McGovern shows in "The Dynamics of Mentoring." Next, Emily Hancock's recollection of and analysis of an especially vexing moment in graduate school offers a fascinating "Lesson in Learning." Our own disappointments as students should not be forgotten, because they may harbor clues to our deepest values.

Paul Lacey remembers some of the students he has taught over a twenty-year career and then uses these recollections to reevaluate his teaching. Linda Clader responds to a tenure committee's request for a written evaluation of her teaching by writing a thoughtful and lively narrative of her first six years as a classics teacher. Her "Self-Evaluation and Prospectus" is worth imitating.

What books can a faculty member who wants to learn more about the development of teachers read? Robert Young provides a generous answer to that question in "Strategies Galore: Resources for Faculty Development." Finally, in "Deliberate Teaching," I provide a brief synthesis of the authors' insights into teaching.

John F. Noonan
Guest Editor

*John F. Noonan is the director of the Center for Improving
Teaching Effectiveness at Virginia Commonwealth University
and Coeditor-in-Chief (with Kenneth Eble) of this series,*
New Directions for Teaching and Learning.

*Writing letters to students about their work provides
special stimulation for teachers, too.*

Letters of Reflection

Richard M. Jones

Narrative evaluation should supply more information than letter
grades, but it is often only a long-winded way of recording a letter
grade. Here, for example, is how I recorded an A minus back in
December 1972:

> Lynette read all of the assigned books and independently read some of Her-
> man Hesse and Carl Rogers. She was also a member of one of the Program's most pro-
> ductive book seminars and a member of the dream reflection self-study seminar. She
> attended the lectures and films regularly. She also attended the weekly faculty seminar,
> which was optional. She wrote a series of autobiographical sketches and two formal
> essays: "The Process of Holding On and Letting Go" and "Knowledge — the Answer or
> the Problem."
>   Lynette's participation in the Program was of superior quality throughout. She
> read the books thoughtfully. She listened and spoke with tact and seriousness of pur-
> pose in her book seminar. She was a sensitive participant in her self-study seminars.
> Her writing was more than competent. In a traditional academic setting, she would be
> placed in the top 10 percent of her class. She is capable of brilliant work, but she did not
> achieve this level of performance, because much of her energy was advantageously
> invested in important issues of personal development. She is leaving Evergreen at this
> time for personal reasons. We would welcome her back with enthusiasm.

The statement does convey more information about Lynette
and her work than the A minus, but I could have decided on the grade
in a matter of minutes, and it took almost an hour to record the information in narrative form. Moreover, the additional information is
likely to be irrelevant (if not misleading) by the time some future employer

or admissions committee reads it. And the writing! Flat, tedious, the more impersonal for being so cautiously personal. That was the part about narrative evaluations that I found the most frustrating: I normally enjoy the act of writing, but writing such narrative evaluations was a god-awful bore. I did not know to whom I was writing, so I could not find a voice that sounded like mine, and in the effort to say only what I was sure was more or less true, it was hard to say anything interesting.

I had begun to reconsider the comparative merits of letter grades when I happened to read a book by Dalton Trumbo (author of *Johnny Got His Gun*) called *Additional Dialogue*. The book is a collection of Trumbo's letters — love letters, business letters, friendly letters, angry letters, duty letters, letters to his children, his plumber, his bank, his agent, his Congressman — which reveals the letter to be a form that invites its writer to engage the English language lovingly. You cannot write a letter in a voice other than your own, nor can you write a letter without first deciding to whom you will address it. If these two barriers between you and English are removed, it is likely that English will, on occasion, make your writing interesting as well as informative.

I decided to see whether narrative evaluations written in the form of letters would restore my prejudice against the grading system. Midterm evaluations, written off the record, seemed a good place to start. Here are two of my first efforts:

Dear Jeffrey,

My guess is that you will be a critic. Neither mediocre nor terrific, but sort of useful. Unless you become a poet . . . or a teacher. The world needs good teachers. In any event, you will have to learn to spell. A lampooner, whether critic, poet, or teacher, must know how to spell unerringly, because a lampooner has to surprise his reader, and you cannot surprise a reader when he's busy correcting your spelling. And spelling includes knowing where apostrophes go. Or is it only that you need a new typewriter? Meanwhile, stick close to Leo. He was probably a lot like you when he was your age (his real name is Francis), and look at him now: critic, poet, and teacher, well on his way to being a wise man — if he isn't already. And tell him I said so.

Glad you liked Trumbo. He did a lot for me, too. Did you notice that I did not forget to put that comma in? And with only one word left to go!

As for your "glibness" in the seminars — well, yes; and you talk too much sometimes (which you know), and you do not listen enough at other times (which you don't know), but, except that you sometimes bore Aynn and intimidate Toni, who also bores Aynn, we love you ever, because you are a nice warm Pooh bear who knows a lot about himself and does not take it all too seriously and does not hurt us when he could and has a lot of good ideas anyway and wants to be loved and deserved to be loved even when he writes "cautiously encourageable" poems to let us know it.

Your reflections on our sacred seminar at the bottom of page 3 (as I took the liberty of numbering your pages) are very apt, and I shall try to remember to read them aloud the next time we gather around a campfire to shoot the breeze. You say that we have not pressed at each other to stretch our thoughts, to carry them out to their conclusions, that we "have shared emotional responses without struggling with the whys of those responses." Do you mean that we are not yet ready for the Sainthood, that we still have some work left to do? You are right! Thank you, Jeffrey. Would you please announce that at our next meeting? Here Aynn has us "sagging" and some other folks have us on some kind of spiritual mountaintop, but you, Jeffrey, have got us where we are at: in need of stretching our thoughts to their conclusions and of struggling with the origins of our emotional responses. Hot damn, I told you that you were going to be a useful critic!

Now, poor man, I have an unpleasant surprise for you. I am not surprised that you could not help wondering what my intentions were in requesting a "detailed, reflective evaluation of the program," because that is not what I did. I requested same of me, your esteemed teacher. I do not want a raise, and I do not need another degree, but I want your reflections on my work for my portfolio, and you may ass-kiss all you like (I can see through such embraces), and when I have this in hand, I shall be yours.

With three units of credit,

Richard

Dear Andrea (like that name),

"Please respond!!!", you said. I shall be glad to.

The area most in need of improvement is not my relationship with our seminar group; it is our seminar group's relationship with me—and with yourselves. You are certainly right in noticing, however, that the combination of my personality and the personalities of those in our group caused the gap between us. Let us look into this like the adults we are and discuss it like men and women. Possibly, we can learn something about human development in the process.

Speak for yourself if you like—and I wish you would more often—but I do not find it hard not to be thinking about pleasing you with each seminar and each piece of writing that I produce, so I find it hard to understand why you should. You may have almost thirty years on me, but I don't see that that makes us less than equal when it comes to matters of pleasing. Let me tell you something: there is nothing you can say, do, or write that will please me as long as pleasing me is as much on your mind as it seems to be. I will be pleased when you are pleased by what you say, do, or write, and you will know it, in yourself and from me, without either of us having to bang a drum.

As for your anger over the pressure that you feel, my "anxiousness" for a "successful" seminar creates, far be it from me to discourage it, but please direct it to where it belongs: to yourself and your fellow seminarians. In the first place, from a viewpoint that I will not be able to share with you until somewhat later in the year, we have had nothing but "successful" seminars. In the second place, it is not from my anxiousness that you feel pressure but from my boredom.

Books do not burden our minds; they broaden, uplift, soothe, cajole, challenge, entertain, confront, and sometimes worry our minds. So, if the books are burdening your minds, don't look at the books in complaint, look to your minds.

I know that you find it hard to be comfortable with me, but I find it easy to be comfortable with you. Perhaps we should engage in a serious conversation. Earnest discussions have a way of melting the barriers of ice that you refer to.

I do not go around hugging girls who are just walking down the hall. But when I come across a girl who is looking for a quiet place to write, I do, I admit, tend to lose control of myself. I'm glad it made you feel good, though. Me, too.

Well, Andrea, if you want to feel more from me, all you have to do is think more for yourself. Believe me, it will follow as the night does the day. I simply will not be able to restrain myself, nor will I try. After all, I am your teacher, about thirty years your senior, have a wife whom I love and two sons who are the apple of my eye, and it just happens that most teachers my age are wired in such a way that their feelings for their students are feelings for their students' thoughts. You can tell that to all your

4

friends in our seminar—and to your goats, too. Because you are wrong: the tenseness will not dissipate before we exchange our thoughts and ideas. It will dissipate only after we exchange our thoughts and ideas.

I accept your respect.

l'chaim

Richard

The students' response to these letters was such that I have continued for the past eight years to compose not midterm "evaluations" but midterm letters of reflection. Here is a recent one which had a particularly stunning effect:

Dear Karen

Do you know that you are the only student in the Human Development program who has met *every* requirement, completed every assignment (including the dream diary), and done so *promptly, thoroughly,* and *neatly?* Now *that* is pretty extreme behavior; as such, it invites both evaluation and interpretation.

My evaluation is that it is just fine. It says that you will probably never have to work at developing good work and study habits. People who do have to develop them (and there are more than a few among your present colleagues) find it increasingly difficult to do so successfully as time passes. It can be downright tragic for an intelligent adult, who has learned to think his or her own thoughts, to have to realize that he or she has not learned the disciplines which make it possible to express and share those thoughts. You need never fear such tragedy. You developed those disciplines long ago. You can take them for granted, forever and ever. You could not lose them if you tried.

Interpretation of this extreme behavior of yours is more of a challenge. There are probably several interpretations that would make sense. I shall concentrate on one: I'll speculate that it is part of a "get by" or "play it safe" syndrome, which can take over even when you genuinely want to do more than just get by or play it safe. That it can take over despite your adventurous intentions is the reverse of the coin: your good habits are so very much a part of you that they can and will take you over any time you let them. Any time you fail to represent your own distinctinve thoughts or choose not to, your good habits will automatically take over and say, in effect, "Here, I will say it in a way that at least will not displease."

Now, if this interpretation is valid, it is clear what you must learn to do: you must learn to make your discipline, skills, and habits serve you; you must not allow yourself or your objectives, purposes, or goals to serve them. Does this imply that you will become thoughtless, lazy, or sloppy? No, those are things that you will forever find it impossible to be. What this implies is that you will have to take chances with the powers of particularity.

What do I mean by this? I think you sense it when you refer to your "high school tendencies" and your "sense of duty" in your self-evaluation. As I said in my letter to the scholarship people, there are signs in some of your writings that you are making progress in your attempt to correct those tendencies. However, in your attempts to date, you have merely been fighting the devil. You must also learn to *play* the devil—do you see what I just did, Karen? The risk I took? I know that I am on sensitive ground here, and I also know that you could completely misunderstand what I just said about playing the devil, because it isn't something that a teacher often recommends to a student. But I chose to take the risk, because when I'm writing I'd rather be misunderstood than not understood—which is what I'm encouraging you to do—this is what I mean by taking chances with the powers of particularity.

Let's look at some places in your self-evaluation where you—or your good habits—chose not to take such chances:

You say that Human Development represented a challenge. Well, if that is all you're going to say, you may as well not say it. I already know that. What I don't know, and what only you can tell me, if you'll risk being particular, is what challenge the program represented to you. What was threatened in you? What was invited in you? Hell, the program represents a challenge to me, too. If you showed me yours, I might show you mine. (You see how readily particularities can lead us into temptation! Risky, risky.)

You say the challenge to comprehend was a struggle, but the benefits from understanding were immeasurable. Well, now you are really beginning to frustrate me, because if ever there was a benefit that I would like to think about, it is an immeasurable one. But you don't let me in on the particular understanding that carried that benefit. Not only do you not let me in on it, you positively withhold it from me. Frustrating. What was the struggle a struggle between? How did it feel? Is it still going on? And so forth.

Studying the works of Freud and Erikson, you say, opened up a new area of "thought and practice." Now you have really done it! The new areas of though that studying Freud and Erikson tends to open, I know a lot about. But new areas of practice? (To what could she be referring? A new way of jogging, perhaps?) Oh, to be on the threshold of knowing how Freud has influenced the practice of a lovely young woman in 1978 and to see such knowledge disappear, even as her "enthusiasm and exhilaration were magnified by eventual comprehension." Oh, I must say to you, lady, that fighting this devil of unparticularity is too much for me. I cannot go on.

So, I'll skip to the last paragraph—where I find that you resolve to strive to achieve a sense of mastery over your weaknesses. No, for God's sake, no! It is your strengths over which you must strive to achieve a sense of mastery. Your weaknesses, poor things, must be cultivated and nourished. They are not yet strong enough to be mastered. Feed them on particularities, and let them play with the devil. This is the prescription that you get from Dr. Jones, here at midyear. Try one particularity per paper, then two, and level off at three for the rest of the year. Give goodness and truth a vacation, and try to stick to the sticky particularities of everyday thought—your own.

Specifically yours,
Richard

When you are less interested in what the student has so far achieved than in the particular process of achievement (or nonachievement) that is mounting and in the part being played in that process by the relationship that has been forming between you and the student, the primary objective is to challenge. Nothing is more discouraging to a student at this point than a dutiful evaluation, addressed to some unknown third person, that drones on about the student's strengths and weaknesses and ends with a halfhearted pat on the back or a mild slap on the wrist, as the case may be. In either case, the student senses that some kind of brush-off has occurred, that the same statement could have been made (and, indeed, may have been made) about many other students.

By comparison, nothing can be more encouraging to a student at this juncture than to receive a candid, well-written, detailed, eye-to-eye challenge to do better—much better—than she or he has been doing. The challenge should be stated such that it clearly could not be made to any other student on earth. The more strongly worded, the better—as long as you can say it with a smile. Put that down as the first rule of letter-of-reflection writing: anything that you say will ultimately be encouraging, if you say it with a smile. Here is a letter in which I only just barely managed to follow that rule:

Dear Steve,

The first time you called me Dr. Jones, last summer when we were negotiating your contract, I felt like looking around to see if anyone else was in the office with us. Gradually, I became reacquainted with myself in those sounds. Eventually, I came to look forward to our weekly appointments, not only because you were doing such good work but because I knew I was going to feel the nostalgic satisfaction of recognizing myself in the words *Dr. Jones.*

When you decided to switch from the contract to the Human Development program, I knew that Dr. Jones' days were numbered. I also knew that it would take some doing for you to reorient your thinking from Dr. Jones to Richard. Which it did, remember? How long was it before "Dr. Jo—uh, Richard" was replaced by a comfortable "Richard"? About three weeks, wasn't it?

In retrospect, something else was replaced around the same time: Steve A., the serious, purposeful, hardworking, productive, if somewhat tight and overly self-effacing student of the contract, was replaced by Steve A., the less serious, less purposeful, less disciplined, less productive, if more relaxed and confident student of the Human Development program. To me, this was a puzzling development, and I want to devote this letter of reflection to the prospect of the two of us puzzling it into a mutually satisfying redevelopment.

The fact of the matter is that your take-home exam, submitted October 24, 1977, was the last piece of written work that matched the academic quality of the work that you did in the contract. Why? I can't be sure, but I think it may stem in part from the influence that the seminars have had on your outlook on education. That is just a strong hunch. Seminars tend to encourage youngsters fresh out of high school to take their thoughts more seriously. Is it possible that seminars have had the opposite effect on you?

I hasten to say that I have not for a second questioned the wisdom of your switching from the contract to the program. You are getting an immeasurably richer education in the program than you would have had in weekly meetings and isolated readings and writings. As you said on several occasions, participation in the program has changed your life. I take this to mean that you are discovering that new thoughts and ideas can have an enriching influence on your personal, social, and emotional life as well as your intellectual life. In the process, however, I wonder whether you haven't allowed the motives and discipline that used to serve the box in your head labeled *school* to wear thin.

I hope these speculations are on the money, because if they are, this letup in academic commitment over the past two months may only be transitional—part of a holistic process of reorienting your life to a new approach to learning, of discovering, perhaps, that learning can be as enjoyable as it is useful, but no less purposeful and demanding for that. In other words, what we may have here is an interesting problem of integration.

How to start solving this problem? One way to stop solving it would be to resolve to work harder and bear down. That won't do it, Steve. That would be a superego solution, and we are looking for an ego solution. Which means that we're looking for a welcome surprise, an *aha* experience of some kind. I suggest that you start looking for this experience in the seminars. I'll be blunt: so far, in seminar, you talk too much and say too little. At its best (and we can only try for the best), a seminar is a time and place for seminal thinking. Seminal thinking can't come off the top of the head. It comes from considering what has been said, then from considering whether one's response is relevant to that, then from deciding whether what you are about to say expresses the relevance.

Am I saying that a seminar has to be somber and sourpussed? Not at all. Only that the humor should come from the combination of ideas, not at the expense of the ideas.

For example, had your joke about Gregor's "apple-ectomy" been better timed, it would have been hilariously funny and we all could have enjoyed it. As it was, it interrupted David's efforts to articulate a layer of meaning in the story that he had been waiting to share and set the whole seminar back a step as a consequence. It was like someone cracking his knuckles during sex.

For example, since we had all agreed from the outset that *Metamorphosis* is anything (maybe everything) but a story about a bug, what was the point of your effort to bring entomological observations into the discussion?

If these critical observations have the effect of discouraging you, I shall be sorry. My purpose is to encourage you to see that seminaring is an art and that it must be approached as such. This seems not to have occurred to you, and the whole point of this letter is to help it occur to you. I'll have some more specific suggestions when we talk.

My hunch is that, once you begin to develop the art of seminaring, the integration that I spoke of earlier will have begun. Then I shall be able to include you among Evergreen's more notable success stories.

Countering the transference,
Richard

"Like someone cracking his knuckles during sex." Should I have said that? I debated it, but I decided to risk it — for three reasons: I was sure that I meant to help, not to hurt; the metaphor had never been inspired by the seminar participation of any other student with whom I had worked, so whatever else it might say to him, it would also say that I was trying to think of him as the unique individual he is; and when the image came to me, it came to me with a smile.

Steve did not enjoy receiving the letter. Our subsequent conference was tense. But he took it, as we used to say, like a man, and later, after his seminar skills had improved, he thanked me for it.

This writing of challenging letters of reflection must, of course, take the capacities and sensitivities of the individual students into account. Lately, I find myself coming on like Jahweh with the stronger students and like your friendly Irish priest with the weaker ones. For example, to our very best student in Human Development, I wrote last winter:

Dear Matt,

I have just reread all of your writings and concluded that you are our seminar's ace student. Everything you say in your self-evaluation deserves to be said, and, with a few exceptions (most notably the first sentence), it is well said. The trouble is, you and I are the only ones who know this.

8

How so, trouble? On two counts, both of which you intuitively anticipated in that memorable line of your writing on *Heart of Darkness* and Teresa's dream: "Differences demand attention!" As you say, your pen is mightier than your voice, and, as you imply, that difference has not received the attention that it demands. In your self-evaluation, you refer to this comparative weakness as "damaging." My first reaction was to see this as overstatement. As I thought it through, however, I decided that the word had been well chosen. Yes, if you do not find a way for your speaking voice to catch up with the development of your writing voice, damage may ensue.

First, it could damage the seminar. What good is it for a seminar to have an ace if the seminar does not know that it has one? Indeed, what good is it to be an ace all by oneself? As a sage once said, "What it's all about is not what it's all about. What it's all about is that we're all in it together." This is what the power of the seminar as an educational device ultimately derives from, I think. Anyway, there you sit, week after week, acting as if all those good "memorialized" thoughts that you have lately been learning to think could have no connection with what is being said, when in your heart you know better. The next time somebody complains about the seminar being disconnected, I may just say: "Blame our star student, Matt, the son of Jacob. He's got the connections (isn't it with all twelve tribes of Israel?), and he's holding out on us." Putting it baldly, Matt, it's a matter of cheating, of not accepting your earned responsibilities. I mean, what do you want for being our ace student? An A? Not here, friend. All you get here for having good thoughts is more opportunity to be a better friend. *Capisce?*

Second, if you fail to make good on the resolution with which you conclude your self-evaluation, the wind may go out of your writing voice. One's speaking voice is always different from one's writing voice, and it is a difference that demands attention. Effective writing improves the clarity of one's speech. Effective speaking improves the clarity of one's writing. Good thinking issues from this ongoing process of mutual improvement.

For example, I agree with you that the quality of your thinking and writing has been mounting at an impressive rate all year long, but there are still occasions when you embarrass both of us with sentences like the one with which you began your self-evaluation. Reread it. That, Matt, is not a good sentence. That you managed to rescue the self-evaluation from it and went on to compose a pretty good document in spite of it is almost miraculous. Dave Marr could tell you what is wrong with it — something in its predication, I think. What I know is that you could never, even if drunk, say that sentence: "With psychology as my primary interest since high school, I had had some experience with . . . ." No, you couldn't speak and you wouldn't speak it. The point is that if you spoke your thoughts more often, you probably would not have written it. Your speaker's ear would have edited it into English, whether or not you knew anything about correct predication.

All of the above, I trust you to understand, is meant to strengthen the courage of your own written (not yet spoken) commitment to round out your very considerable scholarly achievements in your first year at Evergreen. So I shall conclude this letter by seconding your own concluding sentiments in the voice of the geoduck: "Yes, stop cheating us and yourself; speak up."

Ha ha
Richard

("There lies nothing but grief in love and respect for one's father" — from your paper on Euripides and Paul's dream. For Moby Dick's sake, I'm going to get you to tell us more about that.)

And to one of our weaker students, last winter:

Dear Heather,

I have just read your self-evaluation for the fourth time, because the first three readings left me at a loss for words. Your self-evaluation is a remarkable document. It is, at once, an English teacher's nightmare and a quite moving personal statement. It answers a question I've been asking myself all year: Why is Heather in this program? Not only have you given me the answer to that question; you have given me a new measure of reassurance about this modern world in which we live and about Evergreen's place in it. The next time I'm parking at the Sea-Tac Airport, I shall remind myself of the possibilities that the person who takes my money may "know something about human development in psychohistorical perspective," that she may have "liked" *Oedipus Rex,* that she may have understood "half of *Heart of Darkness,*" and that, in any event, she may have done "numerous accounts of reading anyway."

So I'm glad that you are in this program doing workshops, lectures, seminars, and a psychohistory of your mother and reading books you sometimes understand and sometimes don't, instead of sitting in some pre–business administration course somewhere.

As for the time between now and June, you say, "I feel I can better my reading by making myself look upon it as fun and not work." You mean fun as well as work, don't you? I agree. You say, "In writing, I think if I made myself do more of it I might be able to start making some sense." Well, it is not that you aren't making some sense, Heather. It is mostly that you're making only personal sense. You need to try to make *general* sense. From now on, why not try, at the end of each paper, to answer this question: Now, what does it have to do with everything and everybody? I'm not sure that this will work, but I think that it's worth a try. You say, "As far as my speaking goes, I think I won't force myself to speak. I think I will get further if I don't pressure myself." I agree, but I also hope that at some point the general atmosphere of the program will disabuse you of your "terrible fear of saying the wrong thing at the wrong time." It happens from time to time in the seminar, haven't you noticed? And we are still friends.

Gratefully,
Richard

One of the happier discoveries made in writing these letters of reflection was that it encouraged some of the students to reply in kind. For example, from Karen K., this:

Dear Richard,

I just finished *Something Happened.* How could you do that? Well, at least I will not have difficulty being particular about it. I wish I could not be particular.

Reading my evaluation Thursday night was like waiting for my grade in Washington State History in my senior year. The teacher held out. He waved the report card at me from the front of the room. "Come and get it, Kramer. It's all yours." He knew what it meant, and he was getting all he could out of it. When I walked up to get it, he flicked it from his fingers. I watched it sail aimlessly to the floor. I was the one with the pain. He had the pleasure. The card felt nothing. I bent down to pick it up. (It had landed face down.) It was what I expected. He sneered. Was it worth it? Is anything all that important? I never felt the same afterward.

That's how I felt Thursday night. I was being held out on. You were holding back. I knew something was going to happen. It didn't. What was I expecting? I can't really say. Perhaps I wanted to read that my work was more than "just fine."

Friday, when I reread it, I felt totally different. I could see you behind the typewritten lines. You were suggesting things, telling me where I was in need of improvement. You are perceptive. You know what your students need to hear and what they don't need to hear. (I guess I didn't really need to know that you approved of my work; it was more important to know that my work was in need of improvement.)

I would suggest, as you are already aware, that you help me to pinpoint areas of imparticularity. I think that we have reached the root of my writing disabilities.

Now the road is much easier.

I enjoy the program (not particular enough). It's like going to bed in the evening, knowing you did something . . . feeling good and having a nice dream (a little particular, but not enough). It's like having an ecstatic topic sentence, seeing it develop into an even more ecstatic paragraph, and finally into a (hopefully) ecstatic paper (ta da!).

Playing the devil? Well, that is what you do and you are good at it. You take chances with your students, yet it's not as risky as all that.

Thank you for your perception of my needs. I also realized that I could handle it (it felt good). I am not afraid of you anymore, either (it feels good).

Very particularly yours,
Karen

And from Matt J., this:

Dear Richard:

First, I would like to comment briefly on your letter of January 31. You seem to be under the impression that I have connections with the twelve tribes of Israel. Not true. You see, my mother is not Jewish, so I have connections with only six of the twelve.

Second, I resent the phrase "putting it baldly," which appears in paragraph three of your letter. This phrase may not be well chosen in a letter to a guy who has recently said good-bye to over sixteen inches of hair. *Capisce?*

Finally, I beg you to change the opening sentence of my self-evaluation before the document sees the light of day. I haven't slept a wink since you pointed that out.

Tsaright?

Tsaright!

I am scared of everyone in our seminar. My fear level seems to fluctuate a lot, but I am always scared of someone and usually of everyone. I get the willies when I catch a glimpse of Karen K.'s folder. It heavies me out when Ellen produces a work such as her contribution to the psychohistory guidelines. I am put to shame by every barrage of Mastrangeloian words. I am curious about John and Steve S.; what are they up to? Steve A. is a hypnotherapist, which makes me very nervous, and Heather, Karen L., and Sandy are too quiet for comfort. I am scared of everyone. Especially you.

You are somehow responsible for all this fear. I'm not exactly sure how, but I think you are. You are pushy. I push myself, but on your behalf. For example, you write an evaluation in which you refer to me as "our ace student." Very flattering, but then you write five paragraphs that dwell on my weaknesses. Pushy. So, I fear. I fear that if I don't improve, I'll get a less than great evaluation at the end of the year, and this scares me.

I think it all started during our conference in the fourth week of school. You said, right off the bat, "Well, this is a troubleshooting session, and I don't see that you have any troubles that need to be shot." Not a very pushy remark at first glance. Think about it, though. As early as the fourth week of school, you left me no direction to go but down.

Pushy.

From that point on I pushed myself. I had to. I had to fight just to keep the status quo. Things progressed for a while. Then, all of a sudden, you began to push.

You got more and more critical of my writing, and I began to sweat. I thought I was falling.

I didn't want to fall.

I could have developed an ulcer or something.

So I worked harder.

And here is the clincher, the evaluation, in which you bluntly yet subtly put me in my place. You picked me apart, bit by bit, on all levels. You threatened to embarrass me in our seminar by pointing an accusing finger at me, in regard to a disconnected seminar. You threatened that the wind will go out of my writing if I don't learn to speak up more. Low blow, Richard. I've got the willies.

And what purpose does this demoralization serve? What can come of this slow, painful torture? What good does it do me to walk the plank of academia, while you laugh ("ha ha") and poke the sword into my back?

I'll tell you. It keeps me going and growing. I need it. That subtle little foil of yours will push me right into grad school, and I'll appreciate it. (I already do.) That sword is what makes you a great teacher. (A little less than lovable, maybe, but a great teacher.)

You must really care. If you didn't care, all six paragraphs of my evaluation would have looked like the first. Then I'd get cocky, uppity, and impossible to live with. I'd stop growing. I'd feel good, but I'd stop growing. And I wouldn't have the willies; this would be the tragedy.

You seem to right in tune with your students' needs, and you act accordingly. (You must. If you treated Sandy like this, she'd have a heart attack—or worse!) But maybe you do treat us all like this. If that is the case, I can guess why Teresa chose God. His sword is gentler.

The point is that you know that I intend to make psychology a career, and you help tremendously on the road to that career. When concerned with content in my papers, you comment on content. When I embarrass both of us with a sentence such as that which precedes this one, you don't let me live it down. When my writing voice gets fuzzy, you tell me, in no uncertain terms, what needs to be done ("Be our guest," indeed!). And finally, when a habit of mine stands to hurt me as well as the rest of the seminar, you help me to break it.

You have helped me immeasurably thus far. You care, and that matters to me.

Fearfully yours,

Matthew, son of Jacob.

The candor that the teacher earns from students by the example he sets in his letters of reflection does not always result in such good-willed acknowledgments. If I had been unusually perceptive in my work with Karen and Matt, for two quarters I was unusually dense in my perceptions of Mary Jo. Fortunately for both of us, she felt free to bring this to my attention, as follows:

Richard:

I don't feel respect for you. I feel let down by you, and this may color my other perceptions. I feel that you are almost never honest and almost always very selfish.

I never once had a conference with you. I never felt quite so distressed or so close to suicide that I asked you for an hour of your time. Yet, I felt so alone and afraid and stuck sometimes. It would have been very helpful to me if you had invited, or at least seemed to be open to, casual conversation about the subject matter. Willingness to respond to a student's attempt to make the subject matter part of her lived life—not just something reserved for official meetings, even if official meetings are are relaxed as dream reflection seminars—is very important.

In fact, I have felt that it would be an imposition to ask you to spend an occasional hour talking to me about an exciting and enigmatic dream that I've had, about a piece of Chaucer or some other reading that I've done, about my relations with you or a personal problem that is getting in the way of my reading, writing, seminaring, or thinking. I feel that it's horrible for a student to feel such reluctance to impose on the teacher! I think that some of my feelings of distance from the program have resulted from this.

Why didn't I come and confront you with this? I did sort of mention it at a potluck and in some writing. I wasn't frank enough, but I wasn't clear about how I felt and why. And it felt like a huge burden to have something important enough to be worth your valuable time. Anyway, you have allowed and encouraged an open and independent seminar. As you know, your difficulty in getting into Chaucer shortchanged us a bit.

Also, as you probably know, your double message about "write what you want and need for yourself" along with "write what I tell you you should" created a lot of problems. Again, my lack of trust.

Perhaps if I had more faith in the signals of my needs and had claimed some right to your support and guidance, I would have benefited more from you. Perhaps if I were thirty and had met you at a dinner party, I would have felt free to appreciate your being an intelligent and nice man.

Sincerely,
Mary Jo

P.S. I gave this letter to my roommate to read after I finished it, and she said, "Hey, now, Mary Jo, some of this sounds too spiteful and sarcastic." I told her that that was not what I intended, but to try to be honest and clarify my feelings. But then she pointed to my words *important* and *worth your valuable time* and said, "This is sarcasm. Sarcasm almost never says what it means. Aren't you really saying that you hate him for not giving you enough attention." I thought about it and concluded that, if I do hate you, it is as a teacher and because I feel cheated, for not getting enough of the attention I feel I deserve. I hope that this comes through in the letter. I hope that what may seem like sarcasm does not conceal or detract from the honest attempt to convey my feelings.

The two-hour conference that followed soon after was mutually clarifying.

There is not space in this chapter to exemplify the ways in which I refreshed my approach to other kinds of evaluation (transcript evaluations, self-evaluations, colleague evaluations) by putting them in letter form. Some of these are included in my forthcoming book, *Experiment at Evergreen*.

I shall conclude by trying to answer some questions put to me by the editor. In his invitation to compose this chapter, Jack Noonan asked, "What benefits do you get as a teacher out of writing letters of reflection to students? Can you comment on your own vulnerability in composing these letters? How do you know you're smiling? People reading your piece might be tempted to compose such letters themselves. How might someone ease his way into the genre?"

Well, first off, I suggest that anyone who does not already enjoy both teaching and writing should not allow himself to be tempted. If either of these prerequisites is lacking, everyone's interests will probably be best served if you continue to render your observations into one of the time-honored shades of A-ness, B-ness, C-ness, or D-ness. Before reading Trumbo, I was tempted to go back to grading, because (as I now see) trying to write to people by way of trying to write about them had made writing, something I normally enjoy, disagreeable. Deciding to write "letters" instead of "evaluations" solved this problem as if by magic. I had, of course, to read a collection of artful letters (Trumbo's is not the only one) in order to get the knack, but after the first, I knew that I was happily hooked. I wouldn't advise trying to ease into the genre, because that is probably a contradiction. Sitting down to write a letter (as distinct from an essay, poem, article, or evaluation) seems very naturally to invite one to be forthright. I like to respond to that invitation as completely as I can:

> When you wrote to me last year from Massachusetts, I remember thinking to myself, "A good Boston-Irish name, McQuarrie, which is always good for the mix, but I hope he isn't one of those Jung nuts who can't eat his Rice Krispies in the morning without looking in the bowl for mandala symbols."
>
> I have never before known a man who had been disowned by his father; not that I do, I am struck by the vast absurdity of such an act.
>
> I don't think that I ever told you how you got into this program, so I will now.
>
> This is probably a poor metaphor, but I see you taking this program as a person takes medicine.
>
> Doubtless you do not like being compared to your sister, and I shall try to forbear, but I would be less than candid if I didn't begin by saying that my first impressions of you were necessarily colored by the comparison.
>
> Only a man who is at home with his curiosity as you are could have the levity to notice in the middle of his higher education that reading and writing is what it's all about.

As for the benefits that I get as a teacher from writing letters of reflection, they are the benefits of gaining time by losing it. It takes about four times as long to compose a letter of reflection than it takes to write a narrative evaluation, which, in turn, takes about twenty times as long as it takes to compute a grade. But computing grades did not feel like teaching, since the course was usually over, and writing narrative evaluations seemed so pointless and was so boring that ten minutes felt like an hour. Writing letters of reflection can be a pleasure, and most of us, when we are having pleasure, tend to begrudge — not to watch — the clock. So that's the first benefit: Writing letters of reflection confirms the premature wisdom which drew a lot of us into the profession in the first place — the chance to earn a living wage for doing something that is enjoyable.

A second benefit involves another kind of confirmation: Teaching may be the only art that produces no readily appreciable results outside of the fleeting memories of those involved — the students and the teacher. Many students are, understandably, unaware that they are involved in the practice of an art. An exchange of letters that seek to achieve some literary quality as well as interpersonal communication can sometimes help both parties to realize that there is a potentially aesthetic dimension in interpersonal relations.

A third benefit involves the issue of vulnerability. I feel most vulnerable as a teacher when I happen to articulate an individuated impression of a student—an impression that could have inspired a tactic for improving the student's participation in seminar or suggested a way to conduct an office hour more fruitfully or helped to present a lecture in a more personally meaningful way—too late. This happened often when I was composing end-of-term evaluations. Writing a letter at midterm and attempting to do so artfully forces you to articulate your individuated impressions when they can still inform and make everything else that you may have an opportunity to do in your work with that student easier and more effective. The students' increased candor with you and with each other, which is both permitted and invited by your candor with them, encourages freedom of communication in all subsequent student-teacher and student-student dealings. This makes for continued sharing of individuated impressions. As Karen K. put it, "I also realized that I could handle it (it felt good). I am not afraid of you anymore, either (it feels good)."

As to how you know if you are smiling, I am reminded of a similar question once put to Robert Frost after one of his readings. The question was, "How do you know if you are thinking?" Frost's reply: "You know you're thinking when you have a good figure of speech. Like,when I said that Sandburg's poetry was like playing tennis with the net down, I knew I was thinking." *Capisce?*

Richard Jones is a psychologist and writer who teaches at Evergreen State College. His latest book is The Dream Poet *(Cambridge, Mass. : Schenkman, 1979). His forthcoming book,* Experiment at Evergreen *(also published by Schenkman), describes the educational context within which the work reported in this chapter was developed.*

How can teachers increase their own learning in their courses?
Keeping a journal is one way, as this teacher discovered.

Including Ourselves in
Our Own Courses

Annette M. Woodlief

Many people become teachers because they cannot bear to stop learning. After completing formal schooling, they discover that they can learn more in front of a class than they ever did as students. Popular wisdom sees the teacher as an expert who has mastered his or her field, but the truth is that effective teaching often comes from the teacher who recognizes the limitations of this expertise and who keeps learning from every class.

However, the delights of discovery pale for teachers who offer the same course a number of times. They trot out some tried and tested ideas and perhaps a new approach or two, depending on how strongly the students insist on different ideas and on whether they feel in a mood to experiment. It is possible, however, that they can learn more than they realize from interacting with their students, even if the course itself is familiar. A willingness to test one's assumptions about teaching itself, not only the material being taught, can be quite valuable.

Several months ago, I was given a challenge: Write about what you learn this semester in your undergraduate English course on modern women writers. I did wonder how much I could learn this time through the course. After all, after originating the course, I had taught it six times in four years, five short noncredit courses for women from the Richmond area and one semester-long course for Virginia Commonwealth University (VCU) undergraduates after a month-long seminar on course development with our Center for Improving Teaching Effectiveness. The variety of students and the new books studied had made each class a remarkable learning experience. The personal impact of reading literature written by modern women was immeasurable, but the novelty of having my consciousness raised had passed. Since I had taught every book at least once before and already encountered a wide range of students, I assumed that I had almost exhausted this vein of learning. I was wrong—and that may have been the best lesson of all. A journal that I kept during the semester demonstrates that I did have much to learn, especially as a teacher, from this particular group of students. Although I shall focus on what happened in this one course, the lessons I learned seem to be broadly applicable to many others.

Setting up the course at the first meeting was unusually important, since the class would meet for almost three hours only one night a week. After calling the roll, I had the students answer several questions: "What is your major? What interests led you to this class? What do you want to get out of this class? In other words, why are you here and what do you want?" The responses were varied and sometimes humorous, but twenty-five of the thirty-five students said that they had never read any women writers and were anxious to do so; they also wondered why writings by women were so rarely found in other literature courses. (Evidently my quiet promotion of women writers in the department was not as successful as I had hoped.)

Then we discussed the objectives of the class and how the syllabus and the course requirements would help to meet those ends. I emphasized that his was not essentially a consciousness raising exercise or a "women's lib" course (most people have foggy, negative notions of what the latter phrase means); that literature, rather than sociology or politics, would be our primary area of study. Although we would look at biography along the way, the literary characteristics of each work that we read—structure, characterization, imagery, and symbolism—would be examined carefully.

One major question that we would address—and a very open-ended one, since I honestly had no satisfactory answer—was whether these literary characteristics add up, whether women share special strengths and weaknesses as writers. Indeed, is the classification of women writers valid for literature, not just a biological characteristic determined purely by the writer's sex? Do women share certain cultural experiences that encourage distinctive literary choices? Although I did not expect a definitive answer to this question, I did think that our efforts to wrestle with it would be productive.

Since, as a rule, there were few English majors or students adept at literary criticism in a course of this type, I designed the course as an introduction to literary analysis. However, I had also learned not to flood students with new terminology and new concepts, so I kept several handouts on key definitions and leading questions in reserve for the second class. However, I did want students to get a taste of what we would be doing, so after a short break, four poems were distributed, and each person was asked to study one poem carefully and to read the others. An hour of lively discussion followed.

Most of what I learned at this first meeting was about my students. There were five senior English majors, five men, one auditor, one senior English education major, and many junior and senior mass communications and art majors, perhaps ten of whom were studying crafts and sculpture. I should note here that VCU has a well-respected art school, which attracts top students from all over the country. Since one of my hypotheses is that the texture of women's literature is akin to that of women's sculpture and painting and that women artists and writers often share similar artistic and personal concerns, the makeup of the class was heartening. Also, as in all our evening classes, there were a number of older students, two with degrees and many who worked. This, too, was promising, since I had already discovered that college-age students do not often have enough experience as women to understand the emotional context of women's literature, which has been written primarily by women between the ages of thirty and fifty. A class composed exclusively of older students tends to connect the content of the books with their personal experiences rather than to explore the literary character of the books; this can create exciting discussions, but it produces little analysis or interpretation. Thus, a generational mix was especially important for appreciating this literature thoroughly; the mixture of sexes and majors was the icing on the cake.

The discussion of the poetry demonstrated that, while most of the students lacked training in literary analysis, they had abundant, intelligent insights. Indeed, class response unlocked unexpected meanings in one poem that I had taught for years. After class, one student said, "I have never been able to understand a poem before tonight." The poems — by Anne Sexton, Linda Pastan, Marge Piercy, and Adrienne Rich — were not easy. Later, I began to wonder whether the discussion had been so active only because I had said, "Let's see how much we can get out of these poems." The analytic terminology used in the discussion had been introduced and explained by class members. This proved to be stage one of one important lesson of the semester: that my plan to approach the literature exclusively through formal criticism did not suit this audience. Perhaps I had assumed too defensive a stance in reaction to teasing comments from male colleagues, who said, "What do you mean — women writers? That's a contradiction in terms!" I began to wonder if I had been limiting both the literature and the range of students' responses to it.

In spite of these emerging reservations, I conducted the second class as an introduction to formal criticism complete with written and oral definitions of key concepts and questions and close examination of how they applied to the short stories assigned. Several students, especially the English majors, joined the discussion wholeheartedly, while the others bent over their notes. At the break, one woman seemed quite disturbed that she had not approached the stories "correctly" in the paper that she had written for class. She said that she preferred to talk about injustices suffered by the writers, because she was angry. I tried to explain that this was a literature course and that literary analysis would come much easier for her as class proceeded. Later, I read her paper and found that she had written well on the craft of the story, and I indicated this in written comments, but the woman never returned to class to read the comments.

All week, I puzzled over the question of whether I had forced the class too early into analytic response. I knew that I often related to women's writing very personally. Was I trying to prevent students from doing the same? The danger of this class turning into a rap session on women's problems may have existed more in my mind than in reality. Looking at the one-page papers that they had turned in on their reading, I found many perceptive comments but little of the kind of thorough analysis that I had been advocating. However, one paper, written by a graduate student, was too analytic: her eagerness to find hidden meanings led to a complete misreading of the story. Nevertheless, the critical groundwork had been laid. Now I would see what the class would make of it. I had to remind myself that our purpose was to appreciate this particular literature, not to become literary critics.

I need not have worried. As I relaxed my demands for formal analysis and as students, in response to the second class, began to notice individual techniques, styles, and patterns, class discussion and response papers hit the happy medium that I had hoped for, blending personal and critical insights as they did. Evidently most students had not misunderstood my intentions. Although I had said that we should mute personal concerns, the students still felt free to use the stories and poems as a medium for self-discovery. However, they seemed to do most of this in their response papers, while in class they focused on the forms and ideas of the works. For this class, then, starting "tight" and then loosening up had worked. My personal conflict about approaches taught me much about the ideal blend of lecture and discussion for this kind of class as the semester progressed. That is, as I began to see the limits to my professional, formal approach to woman writers, I improved as a teacher.

Another aspect of this lesson involved my initial reservations about the autobiographical element crucial to much of this literature.

The thin line between art and life, especially as drawn by writers like Erica Jong, had long bothered me, although I could also recognize that these personal elements often gave immediacy and vitality to a work. The students, however, had no trouble accepting parallels between actual life and art. Many, in fact, held to the popular notion that a person must have "experience" in order to write at all. This point was discussed at several meetings, and discussion followed the classical dialogue paradigm very nicely. Although we never did come up with an answer to the question of how close to life art can come and still be a work of creative imagination, they and I both understood somewhat and changed our positions.

I discovered that my professional training had led me to prize objectivity and creative fabrication to a point that was sometimes inappropriate for much literature written by women, whose important experiences are often personal and relational. Surely, my scholarly background in American transcendentalism should have prepared me to appreciate the artistic validity of subjective and emotional perceptions, but I found that my judgments tended to resemble those of male critics about some of these writers. Of course, I have not changed my ideas to the point where I now think that Erica Jong is a great writer, but I have rid myself of certain unfair critical assumptions. For their part, the students came to understand that heavily autobiographical works can be too local, too little shaped by imagination, and thus of interest more as history or sociology than as literature. They also learned that the point of view of the narrator is not necessarily that of the author and that the tension between the two can be crucial to an understanding of tone and ideas. We all came to see that a personal experience, handled with care, can provide entree to significant and widely experienced ideas. This discussion culminated when we read Maya Angelou's *I Know Why the Caged Bird Sings,* in which we found autobiography to be under great imaginative control, its juxtaposition of past and present points of view serving both rhetorical and artistic ends.

Surely, it is no secret that a teacher's understanding of the materials used in a course is greatly enhanced by teaching them. Preparation involves the reading of criticism and background, and the reading itself is of another nature, because you must adapt ideas to the class. When criticism is not available—as with some of the works that we studied—teaching the course motivates one to explore the writer's literary choices with care, asking questions like: How is this put together? Why is this said? Why not say more or less? To reread the book with the needs and interests of a particular class in mind can result in new emphases and interpretations. Experience of the book is further intensified in class, as students and teacher share insights and points that they found significant. Often, they reach unexpected and enlightening conclusions as a result of such communal reading. In short, I probably learned enough about writings by modern women to fill a book. More to the point of this chapter, however, I learned much about how to teach that literature.

One dilemma of teaching literature is the differences between the teacher's and the students' experiences of the same book. Sometimes these differences are so great that we seem to be trying to discuss at least two separate texts. To complicate the problem, teachers tend to prefer richly orchestrated works that reveal new dimensions with each reading, while students, who read books once and to meet a deadline, enjoy books that they can comprehend on a first run-through. How can a teacher lead the class to appreciate more complex texts and the opportunities presented by rereading?

Our discussion of Virginia Woolf's *To The Lighthouse,* the first book that we read after numerous stories, poems, and plays, illustrates the approach that I developed to resolve this problem. I had not prepared the students for this book (a rather demanding test had been given at the previous meeting); in fact, I had forgotten what an adjustment of expectations this book demands. As they plow through a book for the first time, most readers are interested in the story, not in mood or character, and they expect a certain neatness and manageability. Rarely are they prepared to be plunged into the consciousness of many characters, treated to multiple recurrent imagery, or expected to treat time as cavalierly ad Mrs. Woolf does. My desire not to shape the students' responses in advance was another reason why I did not warn them of the complexities to be encountered in this book.

The first response in class was a candid "I think this book stinks. I had to keep reading it over and over again just to figure out what was going on. It has no story." Laughter opened the floodgates of discussion: "The Difficulties of Reading Virginia Woolf" was in session.

The gap between my preparation and theirs could not have been greater. During the week, I had reviewed much of the criticism, and I had reread the book twice in the recent past. For many of the students, it was their first whole book by a woman writer, and they knew little more than that some people were "afraid of Virginia Woolf." I had experienced the book as intensely as I could, both emotionally and intellectually; their expectations of a nice, neat "read" were disappointed, and they were confused and frustrated.

We began by exploring the structure of the book. Somewhere in this interchange of ideas, I made the discovery that each section moves from chaos to order, an insight that none of my critical sources had reached. My discovery seemed minor, however, compared to discoveries that students were making as they put together the partial insights into structure that they had had as individual readers. As the insights began to pile up, several students noted that they evidently had understood more than they realized. Ham that I am, I admit that I thoroughly enjoyed pulling a final grand synthesis out of the hat, as it were, but by that point, I had plenty of help with the pulling. As we continued to discuss the book, it became clear that we had all made individual discoveries that added up to a fairly comprehensive understanding. I supplied the basic scaffolding, and we built the rest together.

After class, a number of students swore to read the book again, "now that they knew what was going on," and they chided me for not giving them warning. They may have been right, but I think that the magic of discovery would have been lost if I had. I once taught William Faulkner's *Absalom, Absalom* to a thoroughly briefed class, and the book fell flat. Perhaps I should note that ten students did reread the book, including the one who began our discussion, and four of them "adopted" Woolf as their writer for further reading and writing. In this case, at least, the disparity in preparation did not prove unmanageable, and I learned much about what works in teaching a difficult book to an uninitiated audience.

Toward the end of the semester, I began to wonder just what my students had learned and how it corresponded with my own learning. This question was spurred by a comment from the English teacher-to-be when she reported about Sylvia Plath. She noted the chaotic emotional state that resulted for her from total immersion in Plath's intense poetry and added, "Clearly, Dr. Woodlief hopes that self-discovery will come from our reading. In this case, she should know that it did, and I am a bit frightened by what I saw." There it was in the open; she had stumbled on my hidden agenda. No one was surprised, although I had carefully avoided mentioning self-discovery as one of the objectives of the course. The students had, after all, been writing response papers from the start.

Since these papers were a major mode of learning for both the students and me, they deserve further explanation. Essentially, each student wrote at least one page of analysis, interpretation, and/or comparison as part of each assignment, and students brought these papers to the class in which the work was to be discussed. In effect, they were to come to some conclusions about how the work was constructed and what it said before their response could be shaped by class discussion. I read the papers, commented on them nonjudgmentally (most of my comments noted writing problems and ideas that need substantiation), and returned them at the next class. Meanwhile, of course, the students were anxious to present their interpretations in class for immediate feedback.

The informality and timeliness of these papers encouraged personal reactions, although the students understood that at least one page was to be reserved for fairly objective analysis. Thus, papers of several pages proved to be the rule, not the exception, and personal comments joined analysis. A number of students, either in conversation or in writing, indicated their appreciation for what seemed to them a rare opportunity to examine themselves in light of the reading, especially since this particular literature did invite subjective comparisons.

For the last class, partly to prepare for the final examination and partly to confirm my hunches about their experiences with the literature, I asked the students to write about what they had learned. Not only did I want to compare their responses with my own but I recognized that my learning in the class had been closely linked with theirs. A survey of these papers demonstrates that their learning was related both to the literature and to themselves.

The most frequent comment was that they were delighted not only to know that there were so many women writers but that women writers had written works that were "complex and filled with deep meanings." As one student put it, she had been introduced to a world of reading that she was anxious to explore further. Also, many noted that they had learned to read more effectively. As one student wrote, "I have been forced to start thinking about my reading." Others said that they had learned how to go beyond their initial subjective response to examine the work and ask important questions. One woman who was already familiar with many of the writers used in the class observed that she was reading them better because she had new tools—"better knowledge of the elements of fiction and poetry and a basis for structured comparison of writers." Several students expressed a new appreciation for the "texture" of this literature, which one described as "phases of thoughts and moods of characters, not chronicles of events." On reflection, I realized that, even though I had had a head start, I also had learned much during the semester about how to read this literature.

Initially, I had not expected to be as personally affected by the reading as the students, because I had already traveled that road. Without exception, all the students commented on what they had learned about themselves as artists, as persons, and/or as women (or, for the men, about women).

Several artists said they had achieved a better understanding of the role of esthetic distance in creating literary art from emotions. One wrote, "I responded most to the acute awareness of environment, interior (mental) and exterior, expressed through highly visual imagery." Especially noteworthy were the creative, artistic responses that surfaced by the end of the semester. Several students gave me poems, stories, and pictures that they felt had sprung directly from their discovery of congenial ideas and forms in the reading. Although some of this work was related to the increase in confidence that many women reported, one of the best stories came from a male music student.

Many students wrote that they had learned much about themselves as persons, especially about their feelings and the subtle dynamics of relationships. One man declared himself a "repentant male chauvinist," and two others said that they felt they understood human, and not just female, behavior better.

"I know this is not a women's liberation course, but I have to admit that I have been liberated." This remark was typical of many women for whom identification with the writers and the characters and situations in their works had led to self-discovery and new confidence. One older woman who had long wanted to write was impressed that there were so many talented woman who had faced the mundane problems that she knew without being overwhelmed. She expressed what many repeated:

> I have been inspired, because I feel my horizons have been widened. I don't feel as limited as a person, because I am a woman, as I have felt in the past. I have not definitely decided where I want to expend my energies in the future, but I have more confidence that I can succeed in whatever channel I choose. I plan to expect more from life and myself in the future. What a nice way to end my senior year!

Other comments ranged from "I feel much less helpless" and "I am prouder to be a woman" to "I feel that women have something worthwhile to contribute to this world, and I intend to give my share."

I, too, was more affected by the reading than I had anticipated. Somehow, I found time to turn a dream into a story, my first effort to write fiction. Evidently, familiarity did not necessarily assure immunity from inspiration.

I find that the most significant confrontation with my learning in any course precedes the final meeting, when I reflect on the ideas developed during the semester and write a major discussion question for the exam. This time, I decided to make the question a joint project and asked each student to bring to the last class a question that would tie the course together. As we read, discussed, and compared questions, we saw several comprehensive ideas taking shape. We also dealt with the question introduced at the beginning of the course: "Are there valid generalities to be made about modern women writers?" Although we were closer now to an answer, we became aware that his was a double-edged question that can clarify and unite but that also presupposed limitations. As it happened, earlier in the class we had discussed

Ursula K. LeGuin's *The Left Hand of Darkness,* which insists that the finding and exploring of good questions is far more valuable than definitive answers to such questions. Answers thus become the pursuit of implications and connections. With that understanding, we left our questions hanging in the air.

That exam question—or what I called by now the overwhelming question—was difficult but exciting to write. I found that we had discovered six ideas and literary concerns shared by the writers, all of which transcended differences of nationality and genre (and perhaps also of sex, although that was not at issue here), so I asked students to show how certain works translated these concerns into specific literary terms and to reach a tentative conclusion based on their comparisons. The highest point of the course came for me when I read these papers and shared their syntheses of the course.

In conclusion, it appears that the combination of structured plan with persistent questioning did much to make this course a unique learning experience. The plan involved setting objectives and then using handouts and discussion techniques and literary analysis, selection and scheduling of the reading, and frequent writing assignments to meet these objectives. The structure did not, however, preclude changes made appropriate by developing class interests. Much of the learning resulted from this flexibility, from repeated confrontations between our assumptions and such open-ended questions as "What am I learning?" and "What are women writers really saying and how are they saying it?" Together with my students, I discovered that being forced to think and write about what one is learning is a major route to that learning. Finally, I was reminded that no matter how often a teacher presents a course, the dialogue with each class presents challenges and opportunities that teach the teacher.

Annette M. Woodlief is assistant professor and director of student services in the English department at Virginia Commonwealth University.

*A simple way for faculty members to help each other teach better
without recourse to authorities on teaching
or faculty development.*

One-to-One Faculty Development

Peter Elbow

The one-to-one structure of our project, which turned out to be perhaps the most powerful element of all, was arrived at by a very prag-
matic route. In 1975, we had an invitation to apply to the Danforth
Foundation for a $20,000 minigrant for faculty development, and the
planning group, made up entirely of full-time regular faculty members,
decided that there was no useful way to spend any amount of money if
it involved more meetings. This reflected in part a disenchantment
with meetings and conferences and in part the heavy time demands on
those who taught in Evergreen's full-time, interdisciplinary team-
taught programs. We came up with a plan whereby one faculty member each quarter would be freed from teaching to be a "Danforth
visitor" and spend each week visiting a faculty member who had volun-
teered to be visited. Three visitors were supported by Danforth funds
in that first year. In most subsequent years, the college has supported
another visitor for one quarter of the year (along with the three Danforth visitors). The program has received endorsements from the faculty, the administration, and the faculty union. Each year, more people volunteer than can be accommodated.

By asking for volunteers, we got some very strong teachers to
request to be visited, so there was never any sense that the program
was remedial. It was also crucial to the design that the visitor should be

simply another full-time faculty member, not a professional in faculty development or counseling, and that he or she should be an ally of the person being visited: the visitor's perceptions would never be part of deliberations on salary, promotion, or retention.

In what follows, I will describe how my visits with one colleague worked for each of us. I was the first visitor, and I will simply speak in the first person about my own experiences. Most of what I say will apply to most subsequent visitors as well, although the personality of the individual visitor creates enormous stylistic differences. There have been some structural variations, too; in one experiment, three people were visited over a period of three weeks, rather than one person per week.

Well before the week of visitation, I asked the faculty members whom I was to write informally about what they wanted to work on, the parts of their teaching that pleased or did not please them, the changes that they wanted to produce in students through their teaching, and, more personally, the satisfactions and dissatisfactions that came to them from teaching. I also invited stories about good and bad moments not only as teacher but also as student.

I began each week with a long conversation with the person. At first, I would feel somewhat scared in the middle of this conversation. The person was talking to me so personally, so openly. It was interesting and useful. But was I prying too much? After a few of these conversations, however, I began to realize that I was not pushing people at all. If anything, I was too timid. Instead, it was they who were jumping at the opportunity to talk about teaching on a personal level.

I allowed these long, loose conversations to structure themselves around the concerns of the person to whom I was talking. But I did listen for two things. First, I listened for statements of goals and problems so that I could see what I was being invited to do and the kind of permission that I was being given. I wanted to be saying, in effect, "You set the agenda for my visits and feedback. I will give you only the kind of feedback that you desire. You are the boss." But sometimes it is difficult for teachers to know their own goals. I believe that we sometimes pursue goals unconsciously, and I don't want to prevent intuitive steering. Sometimes after visiting a person's classes, I wanted to bring up a matter than I had not been "given permission" to talk about. Sometimes, I did bring it up, because I sensed that the person would not mind. Sometimes, I asked the person, "Can I bring up something that you didn't ask me to talk about?" Occasionally, I didn't bring it up at all. This, I think, is the trickiest issue of the whole design: the person who is being visited ought to be in charge of setting the agenda, but the visitor should also be able to use perceptions that are not already on that agenda. Theoretically, this is an intractable problem. In practice, however, we seemed to achieve sufficient trust and to exercise sufficient tact and intuition to negotiate these shoals.

The second thing I looked for in these initial conversations was memorabilia, anecdotes and portraits from the person's memory of teaching and of being a student. I wanted to hear about good moments and bad ones, interesting personalities who seemed important, incidents that somehow stuck in the mind. This was a powerful way for people to find out more about their real goals, not just their professional goals. People often wandered into insights as they told me incidents that somehow stayed in their minds through the years. Later on in the week, I would find myself instinctively drawn toward describing the person's present action in terms of these past stories: "You handled that situation just like you said — — — used to do" or "You refused to give that student just what you said you wished that — — — had given you." These conversations opened important doors. Indeed, the writing might have been even more useful if it had followed the conversations rather than preceded them.

Next, I would observe. That is, I would be a kind of companion for a good part of the week's activities: usually a couple of two- to three-hour seminars (our staple here), a lecture or class, an individual conference or two, and probably also the two- to three-hour faculty seminar, where the small faculty team discussed the week's book for their own edification.

Before the final, long conversation at the end of the week (or the beginning of the next), where I brought together my most important perceptions and made my recommendations, if I had any, I usually sat down a couple of times to play back my perceptions of what had happened in a seminar, class, or conference.

I took extensive notes during the initial conversation and subsequent observations. At first, I wanted only to aid my memory — and perhaps also to cover my nervousness — but it turned out to make the process one of mirroring what happened — both in the room and in me — not one of reaching conclusions. Also, I found that I had more to say than if I sat back to observe and wait for wise insights. When I left the note-taking machine on full throttle, perceptions, reactions, nuances of feeling, and even metaphors readily came to mind. In a way, I was free-writing, although I was also leaving out most of the syntax. Certainly I was free-reacting. In the end, I concluded that this had been the most important part of my approach. It kept me from sitting back and watching, diagnosing, prescribing: "Let's see. These seem to be the problems. Here is my advice." Instead, I played back my perceptions and reactions in the mixed form in which they had occurred, which enabled me to give what I have come from my teaching of writing to think of as the most valuable feedback of all: movies of the mind of the observer.

When the person being visited gave his or her permission, I also used videotape or audiotape to record the sessions that I observed. I found that the video was not worth the time, trouble, or expense, especially when we could learn very nearly as much from a small cassette tape recorder with built-in mike. However, even when the electronic process was not a bother, I found it no more than a supplement, certainly not a mainstay of the process. I speak, of course, as one unskilled in media technology, but most of my colleagues who have been visitors have reached a similar conclusion.

Here are some excerpts from my notes. I have turned them into prose fairly similar to what I would actually say when I was playing back the notes for the person whom I had visited. For the most part, I replay them without censoring. I found that by making them as an almost impersonal, mechanical readout of my notes—the moment-by-moment going-on in my mind—my remarks did not seem like implacable judgments or verdicts even if they were negative. Obviously, I never had time to replay my notes of all the meetings and classes that I observed.

From My Interview with Pete Sinclair, My First Week of Visiting

Pete is in his early forties. Balding in front, dark hair falls straight from the rest of his head almost to his shoulders. He is an impressively handsome man with confident bearing. He is originally from—where? His undergraduate work, in English, was at Dartmouth and the University of Wyoming. He is finishing his Ph.D. in Chaucer at the University of Washington. He taught at the University of Wyoming. He achieved eminence as a mountaineer and rescuer of mountaineers. He is an Evergreen veteran who was a member of the original planning faculty. [I leave uncorrected here some of my grosser errors of fact, as a warning to the reader; in fact, Pete had long finished his Ph.D. and had not been a member of the planning faculty.]

He is teaching in a coordinated study program called "From Homer to Hemingway: The Professor's Favorites." Three faculty members, running all year. Mostly classic literary texts. More use of lectures than in past Evergreen programs. An "experiment" for being like a traditional great-books course.

We meet in my office. I wasn't sure that this was a good idea. I'm afraid that I will seem like a shrink. I think Pete said that we would be disturbed if we met in his office—lots of students were liable to knock on his door.

He had done scarcely any writing for me in response to my initial questionnaire. I knew that it was a kind of overkill document, but I did love the questions very much. I was disappointed and, I think, a bit resentful that he had not written. He had just scrawled two pages — two different beginnings to a response. He was unapologetic. He said something like, "Peter, I didn't really have time to do this. It didn't seem worth it. I just thought we would do better talking." "Sure," I said. But it brought up feelings that I often have as a teacher: on the one hand, annoyance ("I gave an assignment and he didn't do it") and, on the other, foreboding ("This is never going to work; I can't make anything happen; I have no control").

These feelings were complicated by the fact that I was somewhat intimidated by him. An original Evergreener from the first planning year, he predates me by two years. More than that, however, he is very confident — even arrogant — in his manner. He seems always to have everything under control — in a place where I find control virtually impossible to achieve. He always seems successful and satisfied with how things are going in his teaching and in his program. That seems unfair and it annoys me. However, my feelings were not so much those of annoyance as of jealousy, I was to realize over the two weeks.

I don't want to overstate these negative feelings. I already counted him as a good friend, if not an intimate one; I think he would have said the same of me. We trusted each other. We liked to talk about issues related to Evergreen, literature, Chaucer, and writing. We enjoyed hearing each other's views, and we respected them.

Thus, my reply was something on the order of "Sure, let's just talk." That is what we did — for three hours. By the end of that talk, I was confident that this was not just a feasible, useful, survivable thing to do but that it was also very exciting.

He did most of the talking. I asked questions, though I did throw in a few of my own thoughts and reactions, partly for the fun of it, partly to prevent the situation from seeming psychiatric or clinical.

I asked if he minded my taking notes. I experienced it as very pushy of me to take notes while I was talking to someone. After a few weeks, I realized that in almost every case the person did not mind at all. In fact, many were flattered to be heeded so closely.

Pete said that the main thing he wanted out of the project was to learn how to lecture better. That was his agenda for the year. He had planned and set up his program with that in mind. He felt confident about his handling of seminars.

I asked him about the outcomes that he has in mind for students. He says he doesn't think too much about what he wants students to get. He is used to students who do not understand him. He hopes that they will come back later in the term — even later in life — and tell him that they have finally understood what he was driving at. Sometimes this has happened, he said.

He does not know why he is so often not understood. He thinks it may be related to his approach to the humanities. His approach: a continual assault on impossible-to-answer deep questions.

How does he get satisfaction? When he comes up with a brilliant insight while he is talking to students. He says that his best thinking occurs in this kind of interaction.

He feels that his lectures are too tight, that he is overprepared. He is not able to let his mind just roll. His goal is to learn to have while lecturing the kind of insight experience that he already has in conversation or discussion with students. He can also get it while writing, but not while lecturing. "I assume they're getting something good if I'm having good thoughts."

He says that at the beginning of a course or program, students tend to be afraid of him. They think he's mean, forbidding. By the end of the quarter, this is gone; students are no longer afraid. He says he's not sure what to think of this. Perhaps it's a good thing; perhaps it makes them think; it certainly gets their attention. But his immediate feeling is that it is not a good thing: they seem to worry more about him than about the book, which is where he wants their energy to go, and it prevents honesty and openness in their interaction with him.

I thought to myself at the time that he is, indeed, somewhat intimidating. [I reflect on this now as I transcribe my notes. He says things with a kind of aggressive confidence that he is correct, and he takes a kind of pleasure, I can see, in saying things in a somewhat perplexing or enigmatic way. He is looking for truth, but he feels that truth can often take hidden, oracular, paradoxical, or parable-like forms. He is not a medievalist for nothing.]

He doesn't know what makes good things happen in class. He says he doesn't care. He distrusts analysis. He is an interesting case of a deeply committed humanist who has become very interested in the uses that he can make of some aspects of social science (psychoanalysis, dream analysis) but who retains a deep conviction that they are ancillary to "real stories"—humanities and literature. I would say now that he loves analysis but distrusts it deeply.

I ask him about his important teachers. When he walked in, he said that he had come to a breakthrough as a result of thinking about who his most important teachers were, and he talked about it in his writing. The fact that it has taken thirty or forty-five minutes to get to this matter in the interview is, I suspect, a result of my timidity. When he told me at he outset that he had been thinking about his teachers, I could have said, "Great, tell me about them." But perhaps because I thought it would lead to depth—perhaps because I thought it might be prying—I tiptoed up to it.

[These teachers provided the meat of the interview. My notes are not very good because there was so much—too much—to write down. We probably spent about two hours on this subject. What follows are the sketchiest of notations.]

The first teacher he mentioned was John Senior. "Super prof." Catholic convert. French symbolist. A kind of preacher. At one point, Pete considered converting. "St. Thomas and I are wrong," Senior once said. Pete quotes this to illustrate the utter seriousness with which Senior takes his own pondering. Looking back, Pete concludes that Senior was indeed wrong; Pete was suspicious at the time, but he loved it.

John Matheson. Couldn't lecture. Socratic. The novel. Not comfortable in interchange. Classes often uncomfortable. But he was witty. He worked you over. You paid for your insights. The people sitting around him always felt stupid. Yet people didn't resent it. Eclectic. "I really appreciated him."

Glyn Thomas. A romantic. Genius at getting students to express their thoughts. "Godlike Glyn." Could make people feel competent. Could take a student's inane comment and follow it, play with it until it yielded important insight. I asked how Thomas did this—very eager to know for selfish reasons. [It was, by the way, simply pleasurable—fascinating—to hear someone talk openly about important people in his past. He was simply rambling, but there was great power and resonance and "voice" in what he said.] Thomas simply had faith that the insight was there to be found if one worked at finding it. He stayed with the student and the comment until it yielded its insight. He would hold the floor open for this student—not let the other students come in, and keep pushing and asking. Thomas made Pete change from engineering to philosophy.

What did these people have in common? Pete had realized that they had something in common when he was writing in response to my questionnaire, but he wasn't sure how to pin it down. It was a very interesting period of the interview while he searched for words and emphases.

These people were unusually forthright. They were always the most learned people around. They simply knew a lot. That is why Pete wanted to work with Andrew Hanfman this year: the most learned, bookish person on the Evergreen faculty.

But while they are bookish and have read a lot, *learned* means much more than merely *dogged* here. Pete is not talking about a bland man who is a walking encyclopedia. The people he named all have some quality of personality or character that shows through the learning—or that the learning is a vehicle for. They are wide-ranging in their learning, and they stick their necks out; they do not specialize in one narrow field where they are safe from attack.

Yet he still keeps coming back to the word *learned*. And the learning always has an important element of background learning, classical underpinning—something going back, something underneath the person's current learning. Roots.

They are all good persons. Virtuous. He almost wants to use the word saintly. He tells me the story of the seemingly arrogant, even negative, Stein, who spent a couple of days hunting down a grad student who had cracked up while preparing for oral exams.

Something here seems important, though I couldn't put my finger on it. There is great force in Pete's talk of the virtue in these men. I sometimes perceive Pete as amoral. He has a characteristic, cynical laugh that seems to say, "Suckers always finish last." He sometimes talks about students as if they mean nothing to him. I am not sure what to make of all this.

He openly characterized his meditation on past teachers as an important new revelation for him. Therefore, I feel comfortable in asking straight out how it will affect his teaching in the future. He is very blunt. He says that he has discovered a simple fact. The people whom he admired are all learned. If he wants to feel okay about himself, he has to be learned. He does not do enough reading. He has lots of excuses for not doing enough reading in the past few years, but he admits that they are all hollow. He has to make some changes. He has to get out of Evergreen politicking. He has to sell his sailboat and use the money to build a little study detached from his house. Pay someone to build it instead of using his own time to build it. He has been putting all his time and money into the sailboat.

But neither can he give up sailing altogether. He can go with others; crew with McCann. He has to have adventure, and *adventure* for him is a more serious word than for most of us. He has always had adventure, either in climbing or sailing. He was a serious miler for six years. He became somewhat famous as a climber and rescuer. He gets the experience of peace from such pursuits, but he thinks of the word *peace* in a special sense, since he told me that it is always accompanied by the experience of fear. Can't have peace without fear. "If you have one real strong objective fear, all the phony ones fall away." He talked about his early childhood and his relation to fear. Something about his interest in the "heroic age," where courage and personality have a premium. No way to fake it. He feels a conflict between his interest in being a scholar and his interest in being an adventurer. But I wonder. It seems that all the talk about fear, adventure, and peace is a metaphor for the quality that he is trying to articulate about those special teachers. all of them seem to have been the kind of scholar who climbs a vertical rock with only ropes and pitons.

From Pete Sinclair's Seminar, One Week Later

Large seminar room. Big pile of fish nets on one side of room. Room must have been used by Pete last year in his program about boats and fishing in the Northwest. Pete and students sitting around. It is not quite 9 A.M. when I come in.

"This is always the worst time. The first meeting," Pete mutters to nobody in particular, rubbing his face in his hands. He engages in some talk with me — sitting across the room from him — about Evergreen history. A kind of conversation just between the two of us, although others are present. Makes me embarrassed, though I enjoy the sense of friendship and closeness implied in the mutual reminiscing.

At 9:10 he closes the door. Threatens to lock it so that latecomers will not be able to get in. I am amazed at the guts of his procedure, but in the end, perhaps because it is the first day, he does not actually lock it.

He plays the "name game": the student on his left tells his or her name, second student tells his or her name and repeats the first student's name, third student tells name and repeats first two, and so on. The list gets harder to repeat as it gets longer. I had never seen this before. Seemed very effective. All the repeating really forces students to remember names. However, I was looking at in a detached way, just sitting there taking notes; I had not been introduced. When it got one away from me, I suddenly realized that they might expect me to play, and that I hadn't been concentrating. Panic. I did have to play. I limped through it, having to ask about half the names. I felt silly.

There were about twenty people. Pete looks at the list of students he is supposed to have; a few announcements or something to adjust role. Some uncertainty, this first class, whether students are in the right seminar — there are three teachers in the program. Typical first-day business details.

I am not sure what to make of the fact that he does not introduce me. Makes me a bit nervous. But I am not prepared to do anything about it. I keep wondering who the students think I am. I am taking far more notes than anyone. What do they think I am doing?

Student starts to ask Pete a question about his lecture of previous day. He cuts her off. "Don't ask about lectures in these seminars. If you have questions, bring them up in the question period at the end of the lecture or at the next lecture. Seminars aren't for that."

This leads him to describe the function of the seminars. "These are *your* time," he says. "Lectures are *our* time." Of course, this does not mean that he isn't committed or interested. Besides, he says, seminar is where he gets to see them perform. This is what he needs in order to evaluate them. It's the only way he can see how they think. It's a chance for them to stand up and be counted. I am taken aback by this approach. It would make me nervous if I were a student.

Nevertheless, he sets out the structure for what will happen. It is their time, but he will decide and determine what will happen. For the first hour, he says, he will be almost entirely quiet. If a silence lasts longer than five minutes, he may say something. One senses that he can hold out that long.

For the second hour, he will ask them to do some writing. It will be personal writing, he says. "If you like what you write, there will be an opportunity for you to volunteer to read it. If you don't like it, you don't have to." Seems straightforward and open in a blunt, friendly way. Then a stinger at the end: "If you are all dull people, the procedure won't work."

I note a slight, ironic smile. Some of it seems directed at me: he and I know each other and can share the irony of what he is about—a kind of openness at being closed, obviously keeping his cards close to his chest. He is just the opposite of me. I want to be seen as an open, nice guy—someone you could never get mad at or hold anything against. I'm struck by Pete's willingness to be inscrutable and scary and the object of anger.

Somehow he manages to begin business by just shutting up and waiting. He had made it clear that what they are supposed to be discussing in seminar is the book. The books are *The Odyssey* and Slocum's book about sailing around the world. Girl brings up something. Rather brave of her to open things. Pete asks her to find a passage in the book that made her have the reaction she just described. I think of this as hard on the person who was brave enough to start the ball rolling, but in fact the way in which he asks her to find a passage is friendly, gentle, fatherly. Conveying both his respect for her as one who dared to start things off and respect for her as an individual: "Yes, I know you weren't expecting me to pounce on you for this task, and it's hard, and you may not be able to find a passage right off [hers was the sort of comment for which it would have been hard to find a passage], but I am sure that you can find it, and I am going to stick with you until you do."

[I ask myself in my notes whether he is being gentler with her than he would be if I were not there. However, as I was writing that, I realized that my comment revealed an assumption on my part that he was mean.]

She takes a long time looking for a passage. Silent. She can't find one. Gets flustered. Tries to give up, to pass. He says, "Wait, try to think for a second: When did you first think the thought that you shared with us?"

Then Pete picks up his book and starts looking through it. Book up in front of his face. Long silence while he looks. I am struck by how this stops all business and makes looking for a passage in the text — in the most concrete physical sense — a central activity for the class. I wonder whether he is doing this consciously, or whether he is only trying to take up time so the girl can stop being flustered and find a passage. [I'm being like the students, always seeing ulterior motive in any random action of an authority person. Probably he was simply trying to find a passage himself.]

The girl, trying to give up: "Oh, I don't know. Someone else say something, please." She doesn't say just that she can't find a passage but that she doesn't know whether her remark makes any sense at all. I note that Pete resists what she's trying to do: he insists on taking her remark seriously. I note that he also could be seen as rewarding the first speaker by taking her very seriously. If so, he succeeds: this girl, and even the thrust of her remark, remain one of the main focuses for the whole three-hour period.

I am struck when Pete closes his eyes at one point in the conversation. Powerful, in a way. He is pursuing some thought in his own head while conversation goes on. Assertive of him. Of course, my unspoken assumption is that the teacher is supposed to follow everything closely. It was disdainful of him to do what he did. I didn't think it was sinful, however. Just intriguing.

From Pete Sinclair's Lecture, Two Weeks Later

"At what point did Penelope know him?" Pause. A student answers from the audience. Wasn't sure whether Pete really wanted someone to answer his question, but it felt good to have someone answer. Establishes a connection between speaker and audience for me.

"She gets gifts. That's her timid action," says Pete. I don't understand at all.

I am moved to reflect on the structure of Pete's lecture: "And then, and then, and then, and then." He's going through the *Odyssey* narrative. But I don't understand why. The effect is to keep us on a string. I look at the students, and I think that they want to get out.

"The focus of the book is on her bed. The suitors, Telemachus, Odysseus." This is the sort of point that I have been missing. I feel energy.

The story is finally over, the *and thens*. "One way of saying it is that there are two levels. She is operating on the conscious and the preconscious levels." At this point he has a different voice. He is looking at them. Until now, he has been talking to the book and to his notes. Only now does he start talking to us.

"That is all I have to say." No summing up, no perspective. That disappoints me. I see now that his last sentence — "He rules the kingdom and house, she rules him" — was the last word of the entire lecture. I feel the brevity as unsatisfying and even hostile to us. Not clear to me what he's saying about the nuclear family. Not clear what he meant by the two examples from the text that he just read. Especially not clear about what all those passages from the text early in his lecture had to do with this conclusion.

Finally, he says in effect, here are a few things left over. Ends with a dribble. I feel let down. I sense hostility in his refusal to be completely clear, to spell out what he has to say.

"I believe that Homer has his hands on something basic — that we might go down the tubes like other civilizations, but Homer has something to tell us to cure our problems." [Not sure that these are Pete's actual words.] This could be his main point. I want it to be — it would be satisfying — and perhaps he wants it to be, but it's not, which makes me mad. He's keeping us on a string, refusing to give.

He asks for questions. The first have nothing to do with what he has been saying. I take this as a sign that I was not alone in failing to understand what he was saying.

"Why did he kill the suitors?" someone asks. Pete gives a very witty answer. Right on the spot. Sums up a lot of issues in the book. Example of the depth and wittiness of his mind. Exactly what I felt was lacking in the lecture. Rich and fat and lovely. Element of surprise. Excellent timing. The lecture was long, a bit disappointing, and had no timing or else bad timing.

Kids keep calling you "Pete" in what feels like a familiar way. Trying to be your buddy. It makes me suspicious.

He gets warmed up and talks with more power as he answers questions, talks to the audience, makes real connections, produces quick, off-the-cuff trains of thought that are not backed up with citations from the text. Nevertheless, they have real power and impact. Everyone hears them, considers them, is forced to see the text in terms of them.

Someone disagrees with his characterization of the maids as unjust. He thinks for a moment and says that the imagery used for the maids implies that they were unjust, and he quotes some of the imagery from memory. I am impressed. When he is pushed, he comes up with evidence straight from the text instead of repeating is assertion with macho assurance. [Sometimes I sense a macho stance that I don't like.]

He enjoys talking with people — not a lecture. The repartee, the wit, the need for a quick answer—it is a kind of contest; that is what he loves. The question is how to get some of that into a lecture.

Pete Sinclair's Written Reflections to Me, Three Months Later

Dear Peter,

I'm going to resist your social scientific impulses by writing a letter that gives you conclusions instead of data. I really don't believe that a process for helping teachers to learn how to teach can be developed that will be independent of the personalities of the teachers involved. However, I do think that you effort to find such a process is worthwhile.

I have learned more about teaching this quarter than in any other quarter except for my very first. For years, I have been hoping to learn how to lecture. I can conduct a class, and can write a good paper and deliver it—that is, I can make a speech—but I cannot do that in-between thing called the college lecture. I think I will learn how to do it by the end of the year. Right now, I'm hitting about every other one.

It has been rough. For one thing, it takes nothing less than an act of courage to follow Andrew every week. I don't know what would have happened if I hadn't had your help. I suppose I would have come up with something, but right now all I can imagine is a total, humiliating disaster. So you see, I have made a big thing out of this—why?

I was twenty-eight years old when I decided to become a teacher. One thing that I learned from your question about teachers who had been role models was that I had liked several teachers and that I had liked them as a class. They were all powerful men, and their power was knowledge. They had very little power over other men and sometimes even less over students, but they seemed to be in command of their minds. Only now do I see it this way. When I answered the question in October, I said that they were all scholars. This has been an extremely important insight for me. When I am teaching a class or a seminar, I only have to worry about my students' minds. I have always been able to read other people's minds, for psychological reasons that are well known to me. For a class, I have predetermined the intellectual content, but the seminar is the students' ball game, and I just referee. In the case of the delivered paper or speech, the intellectual content is established early on, and most of my energy is rhetorical. (It takes me about eighteen hours to prepare a speech.) So why was I not able to lecture? Because I did not believe in my personal authority. A good lecture reveals a good mind working over a body of material; it reveals the lecturer's mastery of the material. Some good lectures are dramatic performances, but that isn't my style. I have always felt that I didn't know enough, hadn't mastered anything. I know that is true of everybody, but somehow it doesn't make any difference.

Now, you would like to know how you helped me to find this out. First, we both have to admit that you couldn't have helped me if I had not wanted to be helped. If we had been interested in establishing a classification of teaching styles with me as one type, I would not have learned much. I had to admit to having a problem. In fact, that's all that I did do. In September, I probably would have said that the reason why I was not a very good lecturer was that I hadn't had much practice. That was enough, because it implied that I had to do something other than what I had been doing.

Your feedback had two parts: you told me what I said, and you told me how you were feeling. Both of those were crucial. I often discarded your account of why you were feeling what you were feeling, but even so, it was useful. I also ignored most of your suggestions about how to do this differently. Let me give you an example. You

38

said that first you felt stimulated by something that I promised to talk about, then you felt confused because I didn't make clear how what I was saying related to that promise, and finally you were irritated that I did not deliver the goods. You suggested that I repeat my main point several times and that I allow my voice to emphasize the critical points. Two lectures later, I found myself writing four issues critical to my argument on the blackboard and erasing them one by one as I raised them. Repetition by sight is at least as effective as repetition by sound, and it doesn't seem like repetition. When you erase something, the audience involuntarily puts it back in their minds, which is a pretty effective way of getting them to do the emphasizing. Incidentally, this just happened; I didn't plan it ahead of time. Andrew and some students said some nice things about that lecture.

The trick to discovering a psychological pattern is to assume that what is done involuntarily is done deliberately and then to ask why. You told me what I did—both what I said and the effect that it produced in you—and that was all I needed to hear to understand why I did not want to lecture well. In a way, I didn't want to be heard and understood, in case it turned out that I didn't have as good a grasp of the subject as I thought I should. In fact, I usually do have a pretty good grasp of the subject, and this is often revealed in the question period after the lecture. In other words, what your honest and critical feedback proved to me was that I was doing a little trick to conceal myself and that the trick wasn't working.

One final and absolutely essential point. It was very important that, through various conversations and from watching you teach, I had learned to respect you. First of all, I had to feel that I couldn't trick you. More importantly, I couldn't have figured all this out if I hadn't thought that I could do better. This is easier if you also think that I can do better. I believed that you believed that I could do better when you told me honestly what I was not doing well. Thanks.

Pete Sinclair

Pete Sinclair's Response to My Write-Up of My Visits, One Year Later

Peter,

I've had a hard time buckling down to this, because I haven't been able to figure out what to do with two facts: on the one hand, your subjective feedback method worked for me; on the other hand, I don't trust it. To put it another way, for more than a month, I have been asking myself, "How can it not matter that Peter made so many mistakes?" Now, I don't mean that your method was only okay or that it helped me some; I mean that it really worked. I got much more out of your working with me than I had hoped. But I haven't been able to get comfortable with the fact that not only do you not verify any of your observations, verification is beside the point. I almost feel that every observation that you make could be theoretically wrong and it would still work. That is almost frightening. It must be immoral. However, under the pressure of your deadline, I have thought of something that seems significant and that enables me to make a few observations.

First, some mistakes that do not matter. I was not on the planning faculty and I finished my Ph.D. six years ago. Those mistakes were fun. They are like jokes that you made at your own expense. I also admired you for letting your projections hang out like that. You didn't know that they were mistakes, but you knew that you had to be making some such mistakes, and I knew that you knew. This is my first important observation: the fact that you subjected your own guesses and assumptions to skeptical analysis and that you did so in conversation as well as in writing provided the model that I, the observed, needed. You led the way into the only critical question: "How am I deceiving myself?" If I had gotten involved in the question, "What do they—

meaning you or my colleagues or the deans or my students—think of me?" the whole experience would have been dreadful. That is the key to this whole activity.

The second important observation follows from that. You did the right thing in not getting much from the students. Only certain kinds of self-deception can be worked on. The ways in which I deceive myself about how my students feel about me are not interesting. We more or less dropped the question of why students seem to be afraid of me early in the year. In your written account of the seminar, you provide lots of data that would be helpful in answering that question, but we didn't talk about it. (Incidentally, I no longer find the question interesting.)

Third and last important observation: I am fairly certain that you and I have very fundamentally different goals for ourselves as teachers. In everything you wrote, only one thing really exasperated me—the phrase "setting Steve up as winner." That remark made me feel that we had totally different vocabularies. Everything else brought the day of the seminar back to me clearly, even though we almost never had the same slant on the same incident. That phrase drew a blank. Eventually, I had a hunch. Jones is a great teacher. Senior and Thomas were great teachers. I wonder if you want to be a great teacher. A great teacher does a lot of teaching with his personality. The student learns because of what the teacher is. I found out fairly early that I was either not cut out to be or not interested in being a great teacher. A person who is not a great teacher and who is not going to become one can do things that would be destructive if they were done by a great teacher. For example, I am often rude. Eventually, the students figure out that this doesn't mean anything. My personality has no importance. I think that some such distinction might be useful in your taxonomy. I know that taxonomies are not supposed to be set up teleologically, but in the humanities we get to do almost anything.

As a not-so-great teacher myself, allow me to speculate on the two. It is undoubtedly better to be a great teacher. Only great teachers change human destiny. Great teachers do have to be careful with their "interpersonal relationships," as we say in the pop-psych business, but they can be wrong a lot and it's still okay. Not-so-great teachers have to have interesting ideas, and it's really better if they are right. If they say things that are not true, these things have to be very interesting. Everything that a great teacher says is interesting, and he has to be sure only that the main thing he says is true. A great teacher also has to be there a lot in some sense, if only in his students' fantasies. It doesn't sound like a lot of work to be a character in somebody's fantasy life, but the great teachers I know are made very tired by their students. I used to talk to Senior and Thomas about anything I thought was interesting. So the amount of work is about the same, either way. The thing that I don't know is how one finds out which kind of teacher one is and whether one has any choice about it. Maybe you will have some more thoughts. I would love to talk more about it.

Second best,
Pete Sinclair

I hope that this view over our shoulders as I visited one man's classes will give a sense of what it was like and encourage readers to try an approach that does not require experts or large amounts of money. I have not described my use of what are, perhaps, the two most obvious tools for faculty development, feedback from students and audio- or videotaping. I did use both tools, but not extensively or well, probably because I invested so much of myself in being a companion, observing, taking notes, and sharing perceptions. I might be able to make better use of these two tools if I were to do it again.

What this approach requires is participants who care about

teaching and about each other and who are willing to look closely at what they see and to report accurately how they respond. The process is built on trust, but our experience leads us to believe that trust flows naturally from the structure of the procedure — as long as safeguards are observed. In my view, the procedure also rests on a crucial assumption about teaching: namely, that there is no single right or best way to teach and that what is good practice for one teacher may not be so for another. Needless to say, the process is enormously rewarding for the visitors as well.

Peter Elbow is the author of Writing Without Teachers *(New York: Oxford University Press, 1973),* Oppositions in Chaucer *(Middletown, Conn.: Wesleyan University Press, 1975), and* Writing and Power *(New York: Oxford University Press, in press) and coauthor, with Gerald Grant, David Riesman, and others of* On Competence: A Critical Analysis of Competence-Based Reforms in Higher Education *(San Francisco: Jossey-Bass, 1979). He teachers literature and writing at the Evergreen State College in Olympia, Washington.*

What can we expect to encounter when we try to alter the way
we teach? This chapter provides a detailed look at
the effects of change on the teacher herself.

The Impacts of Change: A Case Study

Judith P. Newcombe

Professional growth, basically an ongoing process of maturation and development, is often characterized by intermittent activity and change. Although the literature on faculty development is rapidly expanding, very little has been written about what actually occurs when a teacher changes his or her pedagogical style or strategy. Having recently gone through a period of accelerated professional growth, I have undertaken to describe the transition, hoping to present a perspective on professional growth that others might find useful.

Developing Self-Awareness: An Overview

As Noonan (1979, p. 4) aptly stated it, "Most faculty have not learned to learn about themselves." Teaching style is a very personal collection of attributes and behaviors that reflect one's values, attitudes, biases, interpretations, experiences, and psychological responses. Opportunities to discuss our pedagogical behavior or style openly in a nonthreatening environment are woefully scarce. Because how we teach is truly an expression of the self, we are particularly vulnerable to criticism in this area, and we are reluctant to share our feelings and concerns with others. Further, introspective analysis of teaching is difficult, even painful, for most of us.

Nevertheless, however difficult the task of self-assessment may be, it is integral to professional growth. Self-evaluation leads to an understanding of ourselves in the teaching-learning process. In attempting to improve our effectiveness as educators, I believe that we must begin by identifying our own assumptions, examining how they were formed, and evaluating how they influence our teaching. Noonan refers to these assumptions as "the premises about learning and teaching that form the logic of our pedagogy." These assumptions and the resulting teaching patterns are not necessarily visible to students or to us. As the assumptions become known to us, they constitute our theory or philosophy of education.

As our philosophy is applied in the classroom, it becomes a teaching strategy—a rational plan for achieving educational goals based upon theories of how people learn (Davis, 1976, p. 12). Selection and application of a strategy is largely influenced by our personal interpretation of the events and relationships that comprise our educational experiences. While strategy is important, the aggregate of factors that distinguishes one teacher from all others is style. Style is unique. An individual's style is that individual's professional personality.

Teaching strategy and style are largely inseparable, particularly during developmental stages. A teacher's characteristic style and basic strategy evolve gradually and naturally on the basis of his or her unique combination of assumptions. It appears that there is no right or wrong teaching style. However, in order to be effective, the underlying strategy must be based on sound pedagogical assumptions and a unified theory of learning. These three components of teaching style (assumptions, theory, and strategy) should be examined periodically and altered when change would be beneficial to professional growth and student learning.

We often become bogged down in the routines and demands that accompany an academic career. It often takes intervention in our professional lives to precipitate the reflection and insight that allow us to recognize the need for change and growth. Intervention may occur in the form of a negative experience, such as a disappointing annual evaluation, or a positive experience, such as an inspiring event. Once the need or desire for change has become apparent, it is helpful to have a model or paradigm for assessing problem areas and planning changes in pedagogical styles or strategies.

In the case study, improving teaching effectiveness begins with an exploration of personal assumptions. This involves recognition that they exist, formulation of accurate descriptions of individual assumptions, and understanding of how they influence us. When the changes that emerge are grounded in an awareness of ourselves and our relationships, they are more likely to be worthwhile. Finally, the case study suggests possible options for implementing change and explores the dynamics of transition.

Eighteen months ago, I would have been skeptical about suggestions that I make changes in my instructional style or strategy. I viewed programs and resources for improving teaching as remedial aids for relative incompetents. My students consistently increased their knowledge and improved their skills. Everyone seemed satisfied. I did not know exactly why this occurred, but it did not seem to matter. On occasion, something appeared to be missing, and a sense of frustration would surface. Once again, the fact that the problem had no apparent explanation was of little concern. I knew that it would pass sooner or later, and it always did. In retrospect, I believe that my students and I occasionally suffered from an overdose of teacher-centeredness. I hope that the sketch which follows will stimulate other competent traditionalists to reexamine their own pedagogical assumptions and practices. Perhaps other midcareer educators, men as well as women, will find it possible to identify with portions of what I have experienced.

Developing Self-Awareness: A Personal Account

By the time I began to teach, I had enjoyed numerous instructional roles requiring leadership and developed a strong self-concept as a skill organizer and motivator. I had taught swimming since age fourteen, spent several summers as a counselor and waterfront director at the prestigious National Music Camp, been a team captain in many varsity sports, and worked as a secondary school physical education class assistant for three years. I was often referred to by others as a "natural leader." My practicum teaching experiences in college flowed smoothly. "You are a master teacher in the making," I was told. Several pedagogic premises were beginning to take shape. *Assumption: Good teachers are born.*

After graduation, I served as a physical educator and coach in urban public schools. In those years—the 1960s and early 1970s—classes were large and racial tensions ran high. It soon became clear that the key to survival in the classroom was control. An authoritative, command style of teaching emerged as my dominant pedagogical approach. My strategy included daily lesson plans carefully designed for maximum participation. I drew upon my athletic ability and personal influence whenever it became necessary to shift popular opinion to avoid a potential power struggle during class sessions. The regular physical education program was augmented by an extensive extracurricular sports program based on student interest. The level of student progress in my classes was consistently above average, and the extracurriculum flourished. I rarely experienced the major class disruptions and open hostilities that were common complaints among colleagues and administrators. My annual teacher evaluations were outstanding. I had "kept the lid on" in times of dissension and confusion, and I even made progress in program development. *Assumption: An effective teacher controls the learning process.*

My move from public schools to the university level provided opportunities for adjustments in style and strategy. My approach became more task-oriented, involving competence-based objectives and a wider variety of instructional techniques. These changes were appropriate and generally successful, but, viewed in the broad context of the learning experience, they amounted to little more than minor alterations. Another process, which soon placed greater demands on my energy and attention, occurred simultaneously with these methodological changes: I was becoming a specialist. Coming to Virginia from another part of the country, I found fertile ground for sharing my growing expertise in certain activity areas, particularly volleyball. The sport caught on quickly and became popular in recreational activities as well as in classes. An intercollegiate team soon emerged, and I was the coach. I approached this role in much the same manner as I approached the role of teacher. Consequently, much of the players' practice time was spent "learning" new skills, concepts, and strategy. With strong leadership on my part and hard work and dedication from the players, the team advanced rapidly to become a top-ranked regional contender. *Assumption: The quality of learning and effectiveness of teaching depend on expertise.*

As the years passed, new assumptions evolved. In turn, my own interpretation of events, feedback, and measurable outcomes tended to reinforce previous assumptions. I consistently ranked among the top 15 percent of the faculty in annual student evaluations, and I received particularly high ratings on "knowledge of subject matter." Peers and administrators expressed satisfaction with my teaching performance. My failure to distinguish between the roles of coach and teacher was probably another factor that served to reinforce old attitudes and premises. For example, under a relatively authoritarian style of coaching, my intercollegiate teams had amassed impressive win-loss records. There were only two memorable exceptions to the positive feedback. One, which I have previously mentioned, was the occasional feeling of uneasiness — of being "out of sync" with my students or players. This, I rationalized, was a normal occurrence: "Everyone has a bad day now and then." The second was the consistently low rating that I received from students on one item of the computerized faculty evaluation form: "Is sensitive and sympathetic to the needs and problems of students." I passed over this without hestitation, thinking, "I am here to teach, not to mother." I now believe that I misinterpreted both the question and the response. Until very recently, I was confident that my responsibilities lay in cognitive and skill development. What is more, my ratings on such general items as "overall teaching performance" were very high. Surely, this was more important. *Assumption: Effective teaching results from stressing progress and improvement.*

In general, my assumptions added up to a theory based on the premise that teachers are more important than learners in the educational process. Although it went virtually unrecognized, this premise undoubtedly influenced my teaching. The resulting lack of emphasis on faculty-student interaction may have accounted for my periodic sense of disequilibrium. Until I was able to identify my assumptions, I sensed tacit conflict between what was occurring in the classroom and what I thought was occurring in the classroom. This apparently explained my openness to group processes.

During the spring of my sixth year as a university faculty member, I had the opportunity to team-teach in an interdisciplinary setting with a colleague whose teaching emphasized classroom procedures that helped students address their values, opinions, attitudes, and beliefs through interaction with other students. The underlying principle, derived from research in the behavioral sciences, is that opinions, attitudes and beliefs "are rooted in *group* behavior" (Davis, 1976, p. 80).

There are many types of groups and group procedures, as befits the purpose and the setting. Of major relevance to this case study is the role of the teacher in group process. Although the topic, task, and general procedures are established and explained by the professor, the learner is largely independent of the professor. The learning activities themselves are performed by members of the group. Students are expected to assume responsibility for solving problems, making decisions, directing the course of the discussion, setting priorities, and building their own resources, support systems, and structure within the group. In other words, the students perform functions generally assumed by the teacher. In essence, they take major responsibility for the learning that takes place. Once the purpose and ground rules have been articulated by the teacher, he or she becomes a facilitator, unobtrusively guiding rather than controlling the learning process.

Given my own philosophical background, it should not surprise the reader that my initial encounter with group process applied to a physical education activity resulted in something akin to culture shock. This experience occurred when I was asked to fill in for a colleague and conduct a running workshop as a part of the student awareness series offered on our campus through Student Services. My coworker was a master at group strategy and a highly skilled facilitator. As we discussed the format for the workshop in preliminary planning sessions, I soon realized that we approached the teaching-learning process from very different worlds. Suppressing my initial belief that group procedures would cheat students out of a large portion of my own own expert knowledge of running, I tried to approach the experience with an open mind. Much to my surprise, it worked! Here are the notes I made later:

1. I felt that I knew more about the students and their goals, needs, values, opinions, and concerns than I had in previous teaching experiences. This gave added meaning and direction to the workshop itself.
2. The opportunities to share my knowledge and expertise were plentiful. The students asked numerous questions, and furthermore, they were very attentive and thoughtful. This was probably because they wanted to learn the information that was being conveyed.
3. The climate established through group process encouraged open, honest communication and resulted in freedom to express fears and concerns as well as cognitive goals and ideas.
4. I felt a great deal of support and encouragement from the students during the activity phases and the discussions.
5. Attitude changes occurred in most of the participants. I sensed that the new attitudes would lead to significant changes in behavior. Specifically, I felt that most group members would incorporate running into their lifestyles in the future.

This workshop precipitated further investigation on my part into the nature, background, and purpose of group processes. Then, thanks to another coincidence, I had an opportunity to apply this new strategy in one of my own classes. I was teaching a course in volleyball for physical education majors, and there was a three-day period during which the gymnasium would not be available. Rather than using this time for the usual rules and strategy lectures, I decided to use some ideas from the workshop. Since I anticipated that this change of pace would require a good deal of adjustment, I selected discussion topics with care. We warmed up by discussing our recent experiences officiating volleyball in the local schools. During the next two sessions, we moved toward the question of what it means to be a physical education teacher. As the discussion and interaction progressed, students were able to voice some fears they had of the social stigmas that they might face in the future. Feeling support from other group members, they were encouraged to face their own conflicting thoughts and feelings about their chosen careers. At the final session, we discussed the worst possible public image of the "gym teacher." We had a good laugh. We returned to our regular coursework the following week, with a new sense of camaraderie and with improved professional self-images. We were better able to distinguish reality from fiction and better equipped to deal with the stereotypes associated with physical education.

At the end of the third session, we analyzed the behavior that had occurred, noting how different individuals had functioned in the group to facilitate or impede progress and harmony. Then we explored the implications for behavior in group settings as future faculty members. The meeting was characterized by high student interest and response. Students said they they wanted more such meetings in the course and the curriculum.

Not long after, I enrolled at a neighboring institution in a continuing education class designed to help runners prepare for races. I was already a runner, so I took the course to get to know other long-distance runners, to pick up hints and inspirational advice on increasing speed, and to gain the support that I needed to continue training through the hot and humid summer days. The course structure was lecture-oriented and permitted virtually no interaction in class among participants or between students and instructors. The material that was presented was accurate, interesting, and well organized. I was learning, taking notes, often nodding in agreement. But I was neither motivated nor inspired. My training program did not change one bit, even though my new knowledge clearly indicated that it should be altered. Further, I sensed that this was true of other students. After I questioned a number of them about their perceptions of the course and compared their reactions with my own reactions to the running workshop, I became convinced of the value of group processes. They were conspicuously absent from the course.

As the course went on, the limitations of the teacher-centered approach in general and of the lecture method in particular became all too clear. Many of the students sought guidance and direction in making changes necessary to improve their running. For these changes to occur, their attitudes, opinions, values, and beliefs would have to be addressed. It was apparent that the instructional strategy being used was not appropriate, at least for some of the students. Moreover, the course design was too rigid to permit adaptation to individual student needs.

The demands of the setting made it suitable for group processes, and I was convinced that using some of them would have enhanced both the teaching and my learning. In short, the instructional strategy was not compatible with one purpose of the course: to guide participants in their effective development. The strategy was based on the assumption that increased technical and theoretical knowledge would improve running skills.

Of major significance to me was the realization that I could articulate why this course did not meet my needs or the needs of several others. A few months before, if I had been vaguely dissatisfied, I probably would have concluded that the group was just too diverse. Now, I was confident that my evaluation of the situation was accurate. My new sensitivity to students and their learning made me more discerning. I was beginning to grow again as a teacher. I felt excited.

Several months passed between my initial exposure to group processes and the time when I felt ready to use the new methods in my own classes. During this period, I did a good deal of thinking, reading, planning, and evaluating. Gradually, I became more aware of my assumptions and my overall approach to learning. Clearly, change was desirable, and the process should begin with alteration of my assumptions. My teaching style was teacher-centered and traditional. My strategy involved a high degree of teacher control of and responsibility for the learning, meticulously prepared and tightly organized classes, and a priority system that valued expertise and charismatic leadership in the teacher and development of cognitive and physical skills in students

This strategy was effective to a point, but it lacked several key ingredients for meeting the needs of many learners. In order to revise my teaching strategy, I needed a set of assumptions that incorporated my new knowledge and insights.

Old Assumption	*Revision*
1. Good teachers are born.	1. *Modified.* While some traits are innate, many others can be developed.
2. An effective teacher controls the learning process through use of power and manipulation.	2. *Modified.* Power in particular has become less important since I realized that students can take responsibility for much of their own learning.
3. Expertise in subject matter affects the quality and amount of learning.	3. *Unchanged.* However, I did revise my priorities in the method of transmitting expert knowledge.
4. A teacher's major responsibility lies in cognitive and physical skill development.	4. *Modified.* I now place equal importance on affective growth. The priorities in each area, however, depend on the purpose and nature of each course and each class.

One major outcome of the self-assessment process was recognition that more faculty-student and student-student interaction was needed in class. In designing my new strategy, I continued to emphasize the teacher-centered approach, but I modified and supplemented that approach with group methods. I tried to provide a learning climate that made open discussion possible. It appeared that my esteem for my own expertise could also be realized by becoming an expert facilitator, a difficult and challenging task. Control was another factor to be considered. I began to realize that the climate for learning can be more effectively controlled than the minds of learners. I no longer believed that the teacher was the most essential element in learning. In turn, the new strategy that emerged was based on more valid assumptions, it was compatible with a broader range of student needs and educational purposes, and it enhanced many components of my original teaching style and philosophy.

The problem then became one of implementing the change in the classroom. I decided to proceed cautiously, initiating change in suitable classes at the beginning of a new semester. The classes included two sections of "Fitness and Weight Control" in the physical education service program. Introductory sessions, course outlines, and supplementary handouts were designed to establish a climate in which all participants shared responsibility for their own and others' progress. Throughout the semester, activities, assignments, and discussions emphasized the group approach to learning. Although the students were informed that the instructional style would be different from that of most other college courses, they were not aware that it was unique to the class in which they were enrolled or that it reflected a new experience for the teacher. In my other classes, which were predominantly in the teacher preparation program, only minor alterations were made.

In order to assess the value and progress of my new teaching approach, I kept a personal journal and used a more extensive student evaluation system than usual. The journal guided my efforts to implement change throughout the semester. Entries included self-perceptions of my effectiveness as a facilitator, experiences as a participant, and comments on the apparent influence of the group approach on individual students and on the classes themselves. I encouraged regular student feedback. On many occasions, this occurred in informal class discussions or in conversations with individual students. In other instances, discussion topics were consciously designed to induce feedback. Written evaluations were requested at three different times during the semester, and three different instruments were used. The discussion that follows is a synthesis of my journal and student responses.

Each fitness class met twice weekly. Since jogging was our primary class activity, we ran during three out of every four class sessions and met for discussion on the fourth. On running days, the warm-up and cool-down periods were used for the dual purposes of limbering up or stretching out and relaxed conversation. We talked about problems, programs, experiences, and impressions related to personal fitness; often, we planned new running routes. We alternated running in pairs, threes, or as a class. Eventually, we were all running a minimum of three miles per class session at a fairly easy pace, which allowed opportunities for getting to know one another. On group days, the time was divided into two parts. We scheduled a class activity such as a movie, guest speaker, or work in the weight room or physiology lab in one, and during the other, we met to discuss our attitudes, knowledge, behaviors, and self-concepts. Interaction and feedback among participants were encouraged in early sessions, and they had become a natural function of group processes by the end of the semester.

Reflecting on the nature of the events, relationships, and outcomes that characterized both fitness classes, I decided that the group approach was far superior to the teacher-centered strategy for meeting the long- and short-range needs of participants. Most students responded enthusiastically to the challenge of accepting major responsibility for establishing and accomplishing objectives. People lost pounds and inches as a result of adhering to personal fitness programs. Several quit smoking, and some reported a decrease in the use of drugs and alcohol. As group participants, the students became more supportive and confrontive and motivated each other toward greater achievments. A strong sense of unity developed, and many new and valued relationships were formed. Progress was rewarded by recognition and positive feedback from peers. Problems encountered in maintaining diets and exercise routines were openly discussed and generally solved in group sessions. Students were quick to spot feeble excuses for failure to meet weekly personal goals and responded with gentle, but direct, criticism. Changes in attitudes and self-concepts became notably apparent through individual journal entries and discussions. The students had become more aware of their body appearances, endurance, and the physical and psychological benefits of running and exercise. By participating in the class as a member as well as a facilitator, I benefited personally from the students' support and encouragement in my efforts to attain fitness.

There were seven sections of "Fitness and Weight Control" that semester, and I taught only two. In the other five sections, teaching strategies did not focus on group processes, so I had a basis for comparing progress and change. I talked to students who were enrolled in the other classes and occasionally discussed the results of these conversations in my own classes. One student, comparing her experiences with those of a roommate, made a journal entry which spoke for many others:

In the beginning, my roommate and I both took fitness courses because we were getting fat and out of shape on beer and starchy cafeteria food. Sharon's class begins with calisthenics led by the instructor. Then they do different activities that involve exercise, such as jogging, jumping rope, playing a game, or lifting weights. She likes the course because it breaks up her sitting-studying routine, but she does not exercise except in that one class. She knows only two of her classmates by name, and they rarely talk about things related to the course other than how to get through the hour with a minimum of exertion. In our class, there is a sense of pride and commitment. We care about each other and about self-improvement. When I need support or a running partner, I call up a classmate. My roommate is not any help. The bad part is that we can't share new clothes anymore. I have lost weight, and Sharon has gained weight.

By the end of the term, it was clear that the group approach had been successful. Three factors, in particular, appeared to account for its effectiveness. First, the new methods suited the nature and objectives of the course. In any attempt to improve fitness and appearance, it is imperative to change attitudes first. Proper diet and exercise must be valued by the individual before he or she will make the necessary changes in routine. Power to influence these attitudes, I now believe, lies in group affiliations. A teacher-centered approach, in which I attempted to impose desirable values on class members through traditional methods, may well have resulted in short-term change but probably not in long-term change. Although the real effects of class experiences may not be known for years, eight months have passed since we first met, and participants are still dedicated to regular exercise. I have had occasional contact with numerous students who completed the course. They call to make running dates, ask questions about their programs, report on progress or events, express interest in my own program, and offer encouragement. I often see them out running or exercising in the weight room. In almost every instance, the impact of the course appears to have been lasting and meaningful.

The second factor related to the effectiveness of the group approach has to do with sheer numbers. Both classes were small enough to allow for maximum individual participation. Further, by taking responsibility for the learning process, many students (rather than a single teacher) had an opportunity to model appropriate behavior and to influence the goals and opinions of others. Norms and expectations were established within the class itself. Once momentum toward self-improvement was generated by the majority, individual failure or apathy became far more difficult to handle than the demands of exercise. As a result, running became more desirable than not running. Running better or longer was rewarded in group interactions, and eventually the running itself was easier and became fun.

The third and most important reason for the effectiveness of the group approach was the contributions of the students themselves. I was pleased to discover that students are a valuable yet often untapped source of knowledge and experience. When they were given the opportunity and inspiration, they had much information to offer and many worthwhile ideas and insights to share. They also provided support and reinforcement to one another and to me. This comment moved me the most:

> This teacher cared. She cared enough to learn our names, our interests, and our concerns. She helped us to help each other. I like my classes here, and I'm a good learner, but I felt that I was a good *person* in this class.

References

Davis, R., *Teaching Strategies for the College Classroom.* Boulder, Colo: Westview Press, 1976.
Noonan, J. "Fragments from a Journal: Toward Understanding My Own Assumptions When I Work with Faculty." Unpublished manuscript, Virginia Commonwealth University, 1979.

Judith P. Newcombe is an assistant professor of physical education at Virginia Commonwealth University and recently completed the doctoral program in higher education administration at the College of William and Mary. She enjoys long-distance running and is an experienced marathon competitor.

What does it take to be a mentor? This chapter explores the question from both sides of the desk.

The Dynamics of Mentoring

Thomas V. McGovern

In Homer's *Odyssey*, Mentor is a faithful friend of Odysseus to whom the latter entrusts the education, counsel, and sponsorship of his son, Telemachus. The name of the Homeric character has come to mean a trusted counselor or guide.

In the following pages, I offer several perspectives on mentoring. After a brief overview of the theoretical and limited empirical data available on mentors, I describe my own experiences of growth and development with a mentor. The chapter concludes with comment about my work and my hope to become a mentor for others as they pursue their graduate and professional studies.

Theory and Research

In contrast to the literary images that suggest the quality and complexity of the mentor relationship, the *Dictionary of Occupational Titles* (1977) offers a concrete and behavioral definition. The mentor is the most sophisticated form of working with people. The mentor relates to persons in "their total personality in order to advise, counsel, and/or guide them with regard to problems that may be resolved by legal, scientific, clinical, spiritual, and/or other professional principles" (p. 1270).

Our understanding of the mentor relationship has been aided by Daniel Levinson, who adopts a developmental perspective in *The Seasons of a Man's Life* (1978). Using intensive biographical interviews,

Levinson and his colleagues collected data on forty males (ages thirty-five to forty-five) who were employed as academic biologists, executives, novelists, or blue-collar hourly workers. These men's histories were used to construct a set of developmental sequences and major themes. One of the primary themes to emerge was that mentor relationships had been experienced by members of all four occupational groups.

As a man enters the adult world (age twenty-two to twenty-eight), he begins to develop a new life structure. This process involves the exploration of oneself and the world, tentative commitment to basic choices, testing of one's choices, and identification of possible alternatives. Levinson described four major tasks of this phase of early adult life: to form a Dream, mentor relationships, an occupation, and love relationships, marriage, and family (p. 90).

Levinson found that the mentoring relationship most often occurred in a work setting with another male who was usually eight to fifteen years older. The relationship generally lasted two or three years, though it could last as long as eight. Levinson chose to define these relationships by their functional nature. Mentors act as teachers, sponsors, hosts and guides, exemplars, and counselors. In these functions, they help the young man to enter the adult world of work, to learn its values and life-style; these functions also allow them to be supportive in times of stress and doubt. The most important developmental function, however, is to "support and facilitate the realization of the Dream" (p. 98). With the help of the mentor's belief in his protégé's dream, the young man begins to act upon his emerging sense of his own identity and his vision of future possibilities.

In the ideal course of such a relationship, it becomes increasingly mutual, and both men feel enriched by the experience even after the younger man has moved on. Like any intense relationship, however, the process and the parting may be flawed by either partner's dependencies. The protégé may cling too long or rise too fast. The mentor may demand more than he supports if he has not resolved his own polarities in the midlife transition (age forty to forty-five). Either partner can place great stress on a once productive and vibrant relationship. Nevertheless, whatever the nature of the parting, Levinson found that the passage of time allowed the protégé to look back and understand what had been special.

Women and the Mentor Relationship. The men in Levinson's study had almost exclusively male mentors. While he recognizes the value and possibility of a cross-gender mentor relationship in principle, Levinson feels that this factor would only increase the complexity of an already unique interaction. Unfortunately, since there are fewer women than men who can serve as mentors, most young professional women must either rely on a male figure or develop alternative resources for the functions that a mentor provides for men.

In intensive case studies of celibate women between the ages of thirty-five and forty-five, Ellen Rufft (1979) discovered other aspects of the mentor relationship. The ten women in her study were vowed religious whose first job had been in an educational setting but who had made some midcareer shifts to other, nonteaching, positions. Eight women reported having had a mentor relationship, seven with other religious women who facilitated their development in the early years of their celibate life-style. In contrast to the men studied by Levinson, nine of the ten women had no mentor in their teaching occupation. One sister had had a mentor who was solely occupational. One sister had experienced both. In seven cases, the mentor was fifteen to twenty years older than the protégée. "All of the seven relationships with older celibate women who acted as life-style role models have been sustained . . . with an increase in mutuality in these relationships" (p. 81).

Elizabeth Douvan (1979) has written on role models for women's professional development. The paucity of older female mentors must usually be taken as a fact by women who aspire to enter and succeed in a male-dominated professional field. Thus, Douvan feels that such women have three options: to become just like the dominant group, which usually requires the abandonment of feminine goals, to deemphasize competence and professional goals or styles, or to struggle continually to intregrate professionalism and feminine goals (p. 393). Douvan advocates the third route, integration, although she recognizes the almost absolute necessity of some model to accomplish this end. In her analysis of the writings of the early women psychoanalysts of the Vienna Circle, Douvan discovered a particularly workable method of integration: These women used the dominant males as intellectual models and one another as advocates and models for the life-style and professional identity to which they all aspired.

The Graduate School Experience. In their recent book, Katz and Hartnett (1976) identify the graduate student's experience as that of an individual trying to "make it" in the academic workplace. Unlike most apprenticeship environments, graduate and professional schools present an particularly stressful mélange of intellectual tasks and interpersonal difficulties. A student enters, much like the freshman, with a variety of fantasies, stereotypes, and hopes. An incredible amount of information must be assimilated in the very first years. During this time, basic questions continually echo in the student's mind: Why did I come? Will I make it? Is it worth it? In my experience, most of us took on these tasks with a more or less crystallized dream of where the process would lead us, but it is also very easy to lose track of our inner muses among the socialization demands, cognitive challenges, and emotional confrontations.

A mentor thus becomes an invaluable resource to help one "realize the Dream." The Wright Institute study on which the work of Katz and Hartnett (1976) is based reached the following conclusion: "Graduate student relations with members of the faculty are regarded by most graduate students as the single most important aspect of the quality of their graduate experience; unfortunately, many also report that it is the single most disappointing aspect of their graduate experience" (pp. 261–262). The students interviewed were not yearning for complete equality in their relationships with faculty, only to be treated as adults whose aspirations and talents were worthy of their profession.

Summary. The time spent in graduate or professional school typically parallels the period of entry into the adult world (age twenty-two to twenty-eight) described by Levinson. It would seem reasonable, therefore, to identify the four tasks of this phase (Dream, mentor relationships, occupation, love relationships) as also appropriate for the graduate student. However, the academic environment poses particular problems. The rites of passage are often more extended and ambiguous. Autonomy may be devalued rather than encouraged. Interpersonal relationships are often under great stress because of the overwhelming time demands of required scholarship. Finally, one's emotions are often denied, repressed, or acted out because of the paramount importance ascribed to cognitive activity.

Nevertheless, in this environment the future teacher, researcher, or practitioner consolidates a set of values and learns realistic boundaries. Sensitivity to students, the scholar's curiosity, the practitioner's ethical responsibility can all be traced to graduate school experience. I suppose that each of these characteristics could be fashioned independently or, as Douvan described, in interaction with one's peers. Both alternatives to mentorship have become increasingly evident as more and more women and older students have returned to graduate school. Both groups are indeed pioneers as they work out new identities without the benefit of mentors. Nevertheless, I feel strongly that the experience of a mentor relationship is helpful for a graduate student, and I know that it was for me.

The Experience of a Mentor Relationship

Thinking back on my interactions with faculty during my undergraduate years at Fordham University, several people came to mind. Two Jesuit philosophers, Robert Roth and William Richardson, taught me how to think. Whether grappling with Heidegger's writings or learning to synthesize philosophy, art, education, and science via

John Dewey, I learned what it meant to love intellectual pursuits, what the personality of a genuine scholar was like. Both men met with me on a one-to-one basis, sometimes over a text, sometimes over a glass of wine. Both men linger with me as significant role models, Richardson as a "hero." Raymond Schroth, another Jesuit at Fordham, became a trusted friend because of his openness in a relationship that became more and more mutual. The associate editor of *Commonweal*, Ray introduced me to the journalism of Hemingway and Schroth and taught me how to write. When I got married, he celebrated the event and suggested that I write the entire ceremony. To this day, when I read a text, write, or teach a class, I can readily identify the special influence of each of these men on my values and my style. Yet I do not think of them as mentors. My own personality and Dream were not yet clear. As a consequence, I was not ready, developmentally, to relate to them as mentors.

With a degree in theology and philosophy and after two years of work as a college admissions counselor, I began graduate studies at Southern Illinois University. I entered the counseling psychology program with a very definite idea of what I wanted and how I wanted to be treated. The personal attention that I had received at Fordham and some successful work experiences as a counselor raised my expectations. I may have been demanding. At the time, I did not know any better.

I was not disappointed. Several persons became my advocates and teachers. My advisor, Terry Buck, not only acknowledged my need for junior colleague status but satisfied it by arranging several opportunities for me in "early" and highly responsible positions. When I began my practica in psychotherapy, Dick Miller supported my competence and pushed me further. He was not simply willing to reward my basic skills but facilitated my exploration of my own personality at increasingly deeper levels. Both men never wavered in their advocacy on my behalf, nor have they diminished as exemplars for my understanding of a psychotherapist's role and responsibility. Mentors? Yes, I identified them as my mentors. Both of them understood and helped me in several ways to discover my self-concept, primarily by revealing my affective potential. We have since parted, going geographically separate ways. When we meet again at conferences, we find it very easy to engage one another. Even so, both of these men seem to be part more of my past development than of my present and continuing growth.

One person, however, draws together everything I feel about the importance and the experience of a mentor relationship. His name is Vince Harren. I am constantly amazed at the depth and pervasiveness of his impact on me. When I entered the counseling program, I was twenty-four; Vince was thirty-eight and director of the program.

What seems to set this relationship apart from the others is the consistency of how I think and feel about Vince. I recognized him early as my resource person for graduate school. He responded with ever growing mutuality on academic, practitioner, and personal matters. Today, I still regard him as warmly as I did in the past. Levinson said that the essential function of the mentor was "to facilitate the realization of the Dream." Vince provides that support for me. At several times in my early years as an assistant professor, I confronted disillusionment and emotional stress. I have not yet found a mentor in my current university position. When I lose track of my Dream, I remember my first discoveries with Vince of those inner muses whom I learned to trust. It is not memory or a reminiscence of good times that nourishes me, but the conscious recovery of those first experiences of selfhood. I am fairly certain that I was aware of the importance of these experiences in the past. Only now, though, do I fully savor their power.

Very quickly, I experienced Vince as a person in whom I could place absolute trust. I could say anything to him about our program, faculty, or fellow students and never encounter defensiveness, much less reprisal. He was also a public advocate and sponsor. For example, he asked a third-year doctoral student to co-teach my first-year practicum with him. No other faculty member did that. In a first-year theory class, I made a request in class to substitute a subjective paper on certain material for an examination on the same material. My peers were upset with the request. Vince listened to both positions, then left the option open for individuals. I was the only one to do a paper. As a consequence, I was motivated to work even harder, in order not to disappoint him. Years later, Vince told me that he still asks students to read my paper.

The theme of choice was central in my relationship with Vince. Developmentally, the graduate student is at an age when individual autonomy is an important area of growth. The environment of graduate school often provides students with little reinforcement because of the emphasis on required courses, external and undefined methods of evauation, and faculty separateness from student experiences. In contrast, Vince maintained the position that I could make responsible decisions about my education. When other faculty might respond, "Inappropriate; that has never been done before," Vince would ask for the rationale and my goals. He listened to my ramblings, sometimes suggesting alternatives. Ultimately, he told me to make a good choice based upon what I felt was best. Thus, I could always rely on him for unconditional positive regard. He trusted my feelings. I felt respected.

One experience stands out as typical of Vince's style. At the end of my first year, he received a consultation request for a three-day workshop with a group of guidance counselors in Cincinnati. He asked another student and me if we would consider doing the workshop with him. I expected to be his assistant and, perhaps, to do some demonstrations with him. He smiled. Vince expected me to be a bona fide co-trainer, not an assistant, to receive a comparable stipend for the work, and to take primary responsibility for the composition of the participants' training manual.

A week before the workshop, Vince's mother died. After he made his plans and talked with his family in Texas about funeral arrangements, he told us that he would have to miss the first day of our workshop. Once again, he surprised me. Since the leader of the team would not be there, I expected that the workshop would be canceled. He believed that we would do fine on our own. We did fairly well. More important than the event itself, however, was the lasting effect of Vince's confidence in our abilities to be professional, to be worthy of the title *counseling psychologist* while we were still only in training.

Many more examples of this professional collegiality followed that workshop. I made my first presentation at a national convention under his sponsorship. A group of students developed an approach to counselor supervision, and we wanted to demonstrate it. Vince offered suggestions when we asked for them, but he was content to let us bask in the limelight of a well-attended and enthusiastically received presentation. He and I conducted several more workshops together. At the close of a three-day workshop for professional social workers that we did in my third year, the participants evaluated us as a team. They observed that we complemented each other in style and in pacing and that we matched each other in our contributions to participants. I can recall a feeling of overwhelming joy. If others perceived us as equally helpful, I must be getting there. I, too, must have something special to offer people. On the drive back home, Vince made sure that I had heard that message. I had a sense that my Dream, my occupation, and my mentor relationship had reached a new beginning.

On Becoming a Mentor for Others

"A young man in his thirties may do an excellent job of teaching, supervising, and guiding younger persons. To be a mentor in a deeper sense, however, he must first have done the work of the midlife transition" (Levinson, 1978, p. 252). More than once, I have felt some resentment toward this observation of Levinson's about mentors. As a young man in his thirties, I felt that it would not be possible for me to be a mentor for students in our doctoral program. However, when I discussed with several of our present graduate students this notion of mentors and their perceptions of me, some less threatening light was shed on my dilemma.

Since coming to Virginia Commonwealth University in 1976, I have indeed worked very hard to teach, supervise practica, and guide people who entered the counseling psychology program. These efforts have been valued highly by those with whom I work. It has been especially valuable to some of the women, who have identified me as especially supportive of their needs and professional aspirations. Yet some people with whom I have worked most intensely and satisfactorily do not regard me as a mentor. As I reflected on the still unresolved dimensions of the mentor relationship, several ideas emerged.

When I was a young assistant professor, much of my life was consumed in the entry tasks of an academic professional. Am I a good teacher? Will my research be reviewed favorably and published? Does my practitioner modeling seem solid and worthy of imitation? No matter how self-confident or talented the beginning faculty person may be, these are basic questions, and they need answers. Because of my mentor relationship with Vince and the experiences that followed from it, I began to ask some of these questions during graduate school and to receive some tentative answers. After my fourth year on the faculty, I began to let go of the need for answers, even to let go of the questions themselves. On these external dimensions, I had enough data to be able to trust my internal voices again. The behavioral aspect of this search for answers was excessive activity and, often, too many irons in the fire. Slowly, I learned that I cannot be a good mentor if I am perceived to be terribly busy all the time.

A second factor that affected my ability to be a mentor was my need for attachment to others. The attachment/separateness polarity is one of the four issues that Levinson identified as requiring resolution during the midlife period. (Old/young, destruction/creation, masculine/feminine are the other three.) After very warm and close attachments to faculty and peers in Carbondale, I came to Virginia as a stranger. Initially, most of the faculty seemed quite different from me. They were ten years older, had had different graduate school experiences, and seemed to espouse points of view that were different from my own. As a result, I addressed my early bids for friendship and mutuality to graduate students rather than faculty colleagues. I projected an openness to form relationships that were genuine and candid. At the time, this approach seemed perfectly reasonable, since many of the students were as old or older than I and had returned for graduate study after years of experience. I developed a following not of disciples but of students who sought me as a confidant. Because of my own needs for attachment and support, I needed these relationships as much as my partners did. Slowly, I recognized the impossibility of my attempts to be all things to all people.

This current period of my academic career and personal development feels very different. One aspect of the Dream that I identified in graduate school has reemerged—to write my first book and to take the time to do it well. Rather than the frantic pace at which I used to work, I now prefer to write one piece with real quality. Thanks to a colleague who took the time to recognize my feelings of burnout, I have rediscovered the joy of teaching, the very ground on which I based my decision to pursue a doctoral degree and seek employment in higher education.

Much of my emotional energy is now directed toward being a husband and a father to three young children. In this respect, I once again recovered experiences with Vince. One of the reasons why his impact has remained so strong on me was his modeling of an integration of academic career and family life. He seemed to work as actively at both. This topic is one about which little has been written. While women write of their need for models who integrate home and career orientations, few authors address the possibility that men may also seek such synthesis and that they, too, lack good models in this regard. Thus, I am trying to work out for myself a definition and style for a spouse and father who is also a teacher and scholar.

Conclusion

Writing this chapter has been an enriching experience for me. Personal reflections both on having a mentor and on trying too hard, too early to be one myself gave me insights into my hopes and unresolved developmental concerns. As I considered how to draw this chapter to a close, I reread a vintage essay by Joseph Adelson (1962) on "The Teacher as a Model": "When we think of ourselves as we once were, as students, we tend to reconstruct ourselves at the feet of a great teacher—some great man, or perhaps only a kindly and devoted one—someone who infused in us whatever modest claim to merit we possess. . . . There is something in us, almost archetypal, which makes us feel that we achieved our maturity only by taking over the strength and wisdom of our teachers" (p. 62). Do we delude ourselves about the past because our present needs are so strong? Perhaps. I prefer to believe, however, that there is something quite real, special, and lasting in our relationships with mentors. While we may grow out of needing a mentor ourselves, we may grow into being a mentor for others. At critical points of our adult development, we stand to learn much of lasting value when we have someone to counsel us that our Dreams are indeed possible.

References

Adelson, J. "The Teacher as a Model." In N. Sanford (Ed.), *The American College: A Psychological and Social Interpretation of Higher Learning.* New York: Wiley, 1962.
Dictionary of Occupational Titles. (4th ed.) Washington, D.C.: Employment and Training Administration, U.S. Department of Labor, 1977.

Douvan, E. "The Role of Models in Women's Professional Development." In J. Williams (Ed.), *Psychology of Women: Selected Readings.* New York: Norton, 1979.

Katz, J., and Hartnett, R. *Scholars in the Making: The Development of Graduate and Professional Students.* Cambridge, Mass.: Ballinger, 1976.

Levinson, D. *The Seasons of a Man's Life.* New York: Knopf, 1978.

Rufft, E. "Stages of Adult Development for Celibate Women." Unpublished master's thesis, Virginia Commonwealth University, 1979.

Thomas V. McGovern is a member of the psychology department faculty at Virginia Commonwealth University. As a counseling psychologist, he teaches and does research in adult career development and group counseling approaches.

The author shows how we can learn about students' vulnerability
by considering our own.

A Lesson in Learning

Emily Hancock

To begin doctoral studies education, I left an established professional career. Such a shift is costly in many ways. In addition to serious financial compromise, adult status is diminished as the student mantle is placed upon one's shoulders. The efficacy of a staff position in an agency of the real world is replaced by the dependency of one who must petition for admission to courses.

The job I left was that of a counselor in an academic hospital, where I exercised many skills in a variety of roles, some of which are seldom entrusted to a clinical social worker. I had decided to work for a doctorate in human development in order to prepare myself for teaching at the graduate level and to obtain a clearer understanding of the theoretical bases of my work, not to mention gaining the set of credentials that society increasingly seems to require before it will grant recognition that a person is capable of performing beyond the confines of a narrow task.

I not only lost money and status in the move from professional to student, I lost ways of expressing my competence and the recognition that my professional activities had brought. My work had involved many levels of communication with clients and colleagues. Schoolwork consisted almost entirely of reading and writing words — a reduction of the various facets of personal efficacy to a single, linear form. It was hard to maintain a sense of three-dimensionality in the transition.

On the other hand, I had reason to believe that this course of study would meet my intellectual objectives. Virtuoso intelligence is lavishly displayed at Harvard. In the school of arts and sciences, where I took many courses, undergraduates make a practice of dazzling professors and one another. Ideas, literate allusions, polished humor — the atmosphere was hardly comfortable, but it was exciting.

The fall semester brought many pressures. I held a half-time job as a counselor and spent much of the rest of my time applying for grants to support the coming years. I had a new apartment to settle; my son had school problems. I registered in four courses and audited a fifth. A good juggler, I did not miss a single class, but I soon fell behind in course reading and in preparing term paper assignments.

Other students also felt the press of the semester's deadlines, particularly around the end of November. The academic dean of the school was teaching our proseminar and caught our increasingly desperate mood. One evening, she announced that students were encouraged to write a single, substantial paper to fulfill the requirements for two related courses. There was an audible sigh of relief. I felt that I had been saved. I abandoned a project that I had been planning for a course on psychological development theory and constructed another that would serve both for that course and for the proseminar. I submitted this project in early January — one copy to each.

The call came at suppertime. A teaching fellow from the psychology course informed me that I had violated a major university regulation. She claimed that the change in topic from the intended project had raised her suspicions, and by tracking down a footnote that I had altered, she concluded that the paper must be a duplicate. I did not need deny it; she had confirmed her theory with the proseminar professor. Finally, I asked what regulation I had violated. She answered with some sarcasm that any child knows that turning in one paper for two different courses is not legitimate. She expected me to meet with her at her office on the following day.

Confused and afraid, I tried to call the academic dean, a relentlessly fair, strong person who was a warm though hardnosed administrator. I could not reach her, and a long evening of internal debate ensued. Had I misunderstood that one paper could do double duty? Did I seem like the kind of person who would pass off an illegal duplicate and one that was so undisguised? Could a teacher really believe that the white-out used to correct one explanatory note was intended to mask the deception? When the dean, with whom I had a sympathetic relationship, found out, would I fall in her esteem? I worried about discussing it with her without saying that it was her suggestion that had gotten me into trouble, and about how could I preserve the footing of our relationship under these circumstances. Finally I feared that my academic career was about to come to a disgraceful and abrupt end.

When I finally reached the dean the next morning, I told her about the teaching fellow's call. "Tell me what you thought you were doing," she said. I described how I had reacted to her announcement about writing a dual-purpose paper. She explained that there was a whole procedure for using a paper that way, which required the approval of both teachers and the listing of both courses on the title page. She apologized for not outlining the procedure more fully and encouraged me not to take the matter too seriously. The misunderstanding struck her as both minor and easy to clear up. Steadied by her straightforward approach and her acceptance of my good intentions and reassured by her tone and perspective, I prepared to meet the teaching fellow and ask her what I needed to do to complete the course.

At the appointed hour, I asked the teaching fellow how to proceed to meet the class requirements. She shook her finger at me and said, "You had an agenda in this course: to do as little as possible to get to the end of it." I was horrified. I struggled to keep a grip on myself.

I had, in fact, taken the course because it seemed central to my own work and thinking. It was being taught for the first time, by a man who had been gracious and welcoming when I met him before school started. I knew that he had a brilliant mind and a humanistic point of view that seemed likely to provide a rich foundation for the course. Although I felt that the section to which I had been assigned lacked focus and direction, I decided not to change and joined other students to develop some interesting ideas. I helped salvage that section in early December by playing excerpts from a tape recording of two therapy sessions of my most difficult case to provide material for a comparison between two clinical approaches. I exposed all my uncertainties about counseling the client, and I raised questions about applying the two theoretical frameworks. Besides relieving the teaching fellow of responsibility for an entire class period, my presentation provoked many discussions in the succeeding weeks. At the time, the teaching fellow acknowledged that the presentation had served to organize the concepts of the course and that it had been a focal point in an otherwise diffuse semester. How did that prior acknowledgment of my initiative and its beneficial effects match up with what she was saying now? I could not add it up.

I felt jarred by her assault on my intentions. Repelled by her certain statement, woven of so many rank assumptions, I left her office, and headed for the professor's office several blocks away. Bad weather had covered the pavement with ice, hard to traverse in a desperate hurry. When I arrived, the professor was already talking on the phone with the teaching fellow. He told me he could see me an hour hence. Angry and apprehensive, I braced myself in the waiting room. I was heavily invested in this program and needed it to work out well.

The meeting with the professor was far from what I had hoped.

Casting the situation in terms of right and wrong, he showed no interest in my account, but aligned himself with the teaching fellow and proceeded from the assumption of my guilt. While I readily agreed that everything had begun with my hapless error, I felt that it was not right or wrong that lay at the heart of the matter but questions of human decency. His alliance with the teaching fellow prevented him from responding to my feeling that she had attacked my character and impugned my integrity. Instead, he implored me to take her point of view, to perceive how my actions would cause her to believe that I had created a serious disciplinary problem. I was outraged, shocked that they would both conclude that I was foolish enough to maneuver my way through an education by avoiding work and to jeopardize the result with duplicity.

Somehow, I found the presence of mind to recall my objective. I asked the professor how I could complete the course. He gave me the choice of adding a section to the paper I had done or of writing a new and different paper; in either case, the work was to be graded by the teaching fellow. I agreed, on condition that whatever I wrote would be evaluated by him, as I objected to further dealings with a person who had demeaned me so. He insisted that no student had the right to designate who would read a course paper. I argued that the professor has the ultimate responsibility for evaluation. Besides, I saw no reason to try to deal with a person who so flagrantly questioned my integrity. It was a matter beyond compromise.

The professor held fast to his position. I held fast to mine. Hoping to change my mind about having her grade my work, he proposed a meeting that would include the teaching fellow, him, me, and perhaps the academic dean. I saw no point in being present—I had no wish to restore contact with the teaching fellow. He countered by saying that he would agree to evaluate my paper only if I agreed to the meeting. Indignant, I accused him of trying to bribe me and left his office, well aware that it meant failing the course and jeopardizing the fellowship applications upon which my academic future depended.

The professor called the academic dean about my refusal to attend the meeting, and with admirable decency and simple directness, she told me that I had no choice. I was going. So was she. It was not negotiable. The assistant director of the university counseling center helped me to plan for the meeting, which was delayed for some weeks by the semester break and a blizzard that closed school. Our strategy centered on responding to whatever was said with questions designed to reveal the assumptions that lay behind them: that I had been trying to get away with something and that I was guilty of cheating. It was good strategy, but in the meeting itself I could do little with it.

The professor began by stating that it was important for us to work things out so we could all be friends within the academic community. Having assured him well in advance that I would be present only to satisfy the dean's directive and would not provide material for the meeting, I responded with silence. The teaching fellow had been told that I felt that she had impugned my integrity; she said she had not intended to do so. I asked her what she had meant when she referred to my work-dodging "agenda," and she denied having used the words. Her denial so surprised me that I lost whatever hold I had on the strategy that I had intended to use. The academic dean tried to ease the tension by chiding me for my staunch refusal to accept the tendered apology. While I could not help appreciating her disarming combination of humor and truth, this time I was immune to its charms. There was too much at stake.

The teaching fellow explained how she had arrived at her conclusions, checking her hunches, just as one would look up sources before making an accusation of plagiarism. The others nodded in agreement. There was further accord when the dean suggested that I was overreacting, as though they were agreed that what I had done was not so bad but that my refusal to treat the ensuing repercussions lightly was the problem. I was struck by the irony: their claim that I was overreacting was lodged in the context of a discussion about plagiarism — the cardinal sin in academia. My query about how they reconciled such disparities went unanswered. They had settled into a way of making sense of the situation that satisfied them, and they tried to cajole me out of my position.

Bitterly, I invited them to continue their agreement in my absence. What I needed most proved most elusive: to be addressed as a person in my own right, with a coherent perspective worth consideration. Instead, they accused me not only of acting improperly but of having malevolent intentions and exaggerated reactions. Betrayed by their complicity, I was defeated in my hopes of being heard and understood. Close to tears, all I could see was the silhouette of that row of nodding heads. Condemned by implication and demeaned in my efforts, I felt I had to leave that meeting to ensure my survival.

We had met. The situation remained unresolved and raw. The notion that had sustained me until then — that I could carve out something important with this doctorate through hard work and original thinking — vanished. For months, I longed to reinvent the experience, to find a basis for resolving the issue with the teaching fellow and the professor that would leave all of us with our self-respect. I wrote a new paper to complete the course, one that explained the professor's theory through an examination of the attitudes in an educational milieu that form the conditions needed for growth and learning. It was a paper with purpose. He read it and applauded it. He even asked to have a copy of it for his own use.

We are wary of each other still. Comfort has not and, perhaps, cannot be restored. Everything is not all right. If it ever is, it will take a long time. The incident continues to be raised; for example, in discussions concerning my adequacy for extracurricular functions at school. It haunts me. I regret it.

I learned much from the experience, on many levels. I found that when I am hurt I see things in moral or ethical terms. I become indignant, refusing to compromise my beliefs or alter my assumptions even when I am sure to lose. I rediscovered the loneliness of taking individual stands, and I found that rage is one's only ally. I also learned that depression resulting from an injury to one's integrity does not lift in a matter of months. It resists healing, erodes character, and paralyzes academic ambition.

I found that, while I may be unequal in status and power as a student, I still need to assume that I am equal in human worth and dignity. I want school to be a place where I can work in the company of others who are also trying to learn. When I founder, I hope that my teachers will recognize that I am more than the sum of my mistakes and ally themselves with my efforts to regain my balance. I want sponsorship from senior colleagues, a chance to learn from them how to manage the difficulties of being honest with those who hold power in the academic situation. I want to be first a person, then a student. To do that, I need to count on the trust of others.

As I sought to restore my courage in order to continue my academic endeavors, I was struck by the similarities between teaching, counseling, and parenting. Making one's way in life, whether as a student, a client, or a child, requires one to abandon familiar patterns and to try new ones — and the transitions between the familiar patterns and the new ones often upset one's balance and engender feelings of vulnerability. In counseling, the client invests the consultant with authority, regardless of whether or not the consultant is an authoritative person by nature, simply because the client needs help and hopes that consultation will produce it. The consultant who does not abuse this power helps the client to invest it in the client's own self. Although counselors are trained to make self-discovery easier, they are not necessarily morally or intellectually superior to their clients. The inequality of counselor and client is an artifact of their professional relationship. In some ways, clients know themselves better than a consultant ever can. All that a consultant can do is apply skills to the clients' difficulties. As clients master these skills, they gain faith in their own abilities. The counselor helps to clarify the meaning of the client's experience and at the same time establishes the client as the architect of this experience. Counseling shows that the disparity between consultant and client is situational.

The classroom has some of the same characteristics, notably a situational imbalance of power. The student who enrolls in an academic program is placed in a subordinate position. Within months, absolute truths are traded for relative questions—though the latter may offer little comfort. Unexamined convictions are replaced with intellectual inquiry, and the student feels in flux—in some cases, adrift. At least in the beginning, the student's awe of faculty, authority, the institution itself, can intensify the student's insecurity. But the discrepancy between student and faculty does not stem from inherent, immutable differences in intellect or human worth. The objective of education is to bring students to parity with those from whom they learn, so that they, like clients, can apply skills to their chosen areas of concern. The discrepancy between students and their instructors lies in the distribution of power, which can eventually be equalized.

Is it not so also with parents and their children? Babies are far more helpless than clients or students, for they depend upon their parents for survival itself. But parents care for their children with an awareness that their dominance is temporary and situational. While parents will always be senior to their offspring, their children's eventual maturity can nullify the inequalities between them—as it can between clients and counselors and between students and teachers.

As I reflected on what had happened, trying to learn from it so that I could be a better educator, I concluded that counselor, teacher, and parent alike should feel obligated to take steps to mitigate the imbalance of power, as they are the ones who can act to do so. We who teach must devise ways to help students define their objectives, identify methods of investigation with which to pursue them, and develop the professional skills that they need for their chosen fields—all with a spirit that conveys our respect for them as persons. To do so, we must act from the premise that the educational framework exists for our students' purposes and start from their understanding of and questions about the intellectual matters at hand. When a professor encourages students to see how the academic material pertains to their experiences and to follow out individual lines of inquiry, students become the authors of experience as well as of scholarly papers. Like the counselor, the professor is engaged on the student's behalf, and the work they do together is dependent on some combination of the student's individual motivation with the professor's stance toward it. When a student uses theory to capture experience, learning is integrated and new perspectives emerge. Thereafter, the student, like the client, can direct the use of abstraction and suit it to individual purposes. As a teacher, I work to confirm the subjective experience of learning and changing. I want to help students to make the material their own, and I want to make explicit the artificial inequality of our situation. While I view these standards as idealistic, I do not expect to function well without ideals. I need them.

I can provide no formula to ensure that education will be conducted more humanely for all concerned. But, like other developmental contexts, educational settings promote growth where the give-and-take is spontaneous and authentic and where it is based on benevolent assumptions about people's work and objectives. This requires a value system, explicit construction of a constellation of power in which junior and senior members of the community are equal in humanity, if not in status. The particulars of the events that I have narrated provide some illustration. The dean's invitation, "Tell me what you thought you were doing," told me that, in making a judgment, my intentions were important and valid aspects of the situation. She treated me not as the problem but as a subject worth understanding, and she made it her business to inquire without insinuation. In doing so, she implied that I had a perspective of my own, one that she wished to explore and take into account.

These events clarified my attitudes toward teaching and toward education itself. I found that one cannot separate experience from scholarship. Feelings and intentions are just as much facts as manifest acts, and inquiry into motives and hopes is worth more than accusation where learning is the goal. If student and teacher regard each other as serious and competent people, the educational process has the potential to change them both—and to foster original thinking. Good teaching, like good counseling and good parenting, begins by asking questions and moves forward from a shared perspective based on mutual regard. Unless integrity is the currency of exchange between teacher and student, education can evoke shame instead of pride—a travesty of human values.

This learning cost.

Emily Hancock is a doctoral candidate in human development at Harvard University Graduate School of Education, a member of the editorial board of the Harvard Educational Review, *a Danforth Fellow, and a recipient of a Woodrow Wilson Grant in women's studies.*

Effective teaching grows from a double dialogue: the professional
with the discipline, and the teacher with the student.
Graduate education prepares us only for the first,
but our richest development as teachers can come
from addressing the developmental needs
of our students through the medium
of discipline.

Teaching as a
Double Dialogue

Paul A. Lacey

In June 1980, I completed my twentieth year of teaching, which means
that I have been a teacher longer than I was a student. (Had I not
dropped out of kindergarten after a month, I would just be breaking
even in time spent on either side of the teacher's desk.) That is worth
reflecting on. When we begin teaching, we have a lifetime of teaching
models to influence us; consciously and unconsciously, we teach like
our favorite or most impressive teachers. We have seen an enormous
amount of teaching and participated in an enormous amount of learning, yet we know little about the optimum conditions for learning or
how a teacher can best communicate information, or even whether
transmission of information is central or peripheral to the teaching-
learning process.

In these past several years—during which I have been an
administrator concerned with faculty development, a teacher looking
at some of the results of my own teaching, and a man coming into my
middle forties—I have had many reminders of how much experience of
teaching and learning I have and of how little I know about either. I am
now in my second year as a faculty consultant on teaching and learning
at Fordham College, in which capacity I visit classes and observe lectures and discussions. I find myself stimulated by watching my colleagues, and I learn a lot from them, but I also find myself wondering

whether I know what I am observing. This fall, a colleague asked me to assess his lectures for clarity and comprehensiveness. The notes I took in two weeks of classes turned out to be almost perfect transcripts of his lecture notes, and I am sure that I could pass any test that required knowledge and understanding of the material. But a high percentage of students have trouble with the course, and while I sat taking notes, some people chatted and others never took a note. I found myself wondering what clues these students were getting to tell them that taking notes was unnecessary. What were they doing in class? Were they learning? If so, how? If not, why not? Later, I watched students studying for a test. That is, they turned pages and underlined passages. Were they learning? Apparently, even they did not know. Two of them predicted they would fail; in fact, one got an A and the other, a D. One seems to have learned the material; the other seems only to have learned her own situation. But was this an accurate perception?

Examining these questions has led me back to a passage from Erik Erikson's *Insight and Responsibility* that has come to mean a great deal to me: "*Care* is a quality essential for psychosocial evolution, for we are the teaching species. . . . Only man . . . can and must extend his solicitude over the long, parallel and overlapping childhoods of numerous offspring united in households and communities" (p. 130).

We are the teaching species because we do very little by instinct, and we must therefore depend on education to survive. However, Erikson emphasizes the teaching over the learning, almost as though the capacity to teach accounts more for our survival than the capacity to learn. Learning can be a solitary activity; teaching must always be social. Teaching is a complex relationship with other people, which may range from instruction, indoctrination, or drilling to the most profound intellectual and spiritual companionship. In some ways, our capacity to be learners depends on our capacity to take the responsibility for others that is implied in teaching. Erikson says only humans can and must extend solicitude over long, parallel, and overlapping generations.

Reflecting thus on Erikson's description of the teaching species led me to consider two related questions: What has my development been like since I started teaching? What has the development of my students been like as a result of studying with me or in the institution that I have been part of? In what follows, I offer partial answers to those questions.

Starting to teach in the early sixties was very heady. For a time, it seemed possible to be virtually all good things at once. We could pay homage to the values of liberal education while in fact we were refining a major that had been designed only to send people to graduate school. Our best students were admitted to good graduate schools and taught at excellent colleges; those who were not interested in graduate school were rather quiet or apologetic about why they were majoring with us. We professors were engaging in self-replication while calling it rigorous liberal education. Few people complained.

I dwell on this because I know that, by every measure usually applied, I was a very good teacher in those days. Rigorous, a hard marker, I packed a good deal into my courses, but I was also fond of my students and sympathetic to their personal needs. Yet I now look back on that time with some sorrow and regret, because in some of the most important aspects of teaching I was totally ignorant. I was so unconscious of the assumptions that we were making about the aims of education that I helped to make a number of fine men and women feel like failures when they could not or did not want to choose graduate school, teaching, and research as a way of life. That is to say, because I was pursuing my professional goals uncritically and unreflectively, my own development was doing damage to the development of others.

In the past few years, I have corresponded with and visited a number of students from that period, people who are now doing impressive things with their lives but who still speak apologetically about their time as students. One, a skillful professional writer whom I treasured when she was in my classes, wrote on the occasion of her tenth class reunion that I probably would not remember her, but, like a Graham Greene character, she had tried to be faithful to her school in her failure. I replied at some length, telling her all the things I remembered about her, including what I had written on her final first-year paper and how she had celebrated her last, late paper in college by stealing daisies out of a neighbor's yard to distribute to the students having tea with us in our living room at midnight in early June. I also asked what all that Graham Greene nonsense was about, and that began a wonderful correspondence which still continues. My student studied literature because she loved to read and write, but she never intended to go to graduate school. But, as she wrote, "Those of us who weren't going to graduate school were like daughters among the Chinese. We knew we were loved, but no one knew what to do with us."

Another graduate of that time, a prominent social analyst, has told me that she graduated thinking of herself as not intellectual enough to do graduate work in her major and that she considered her involvement in social work as evidence of her failure. More recently, we had a visit from a man who has done excellent work at a first-rate graduate school. While preparing for his qualifying examinations, he began to teach kindergarten, as a break from pressure. He discovered that he loved the work and the age group, and although he will complete his degree and quite possibly publish in his original field, he has resolved to make his career teaching kindergarten. He and his wife did not return to the college for eight years, because they were afraid that we would misunderstand him and think he had failed. He said to us, "We knew the place would understand—the trees, the meetinghouse—but we didn't want to risk losing the respect of our teachers."

I could offer a dozen similar examples of apologetic you-don't-remember-me's from people I cherished, midnight confessions of the fear of seeming a failure, tearful self-disparagement. What such things tell me is that, while I was extending my own professional development along lines established by graduate school thinking, I was stunting the development of some of my students, and because teaching is what it is, I may have been doing the greatest damage to those people with whom my bonds of affection were strongest.

What is more, as I look back, I realize that some of the most valuable contributions to my development as a teacher and, I believe, as a person were so unorthodox that their value could not be recognized at the time. Two things that I now consider crucial to my development date from those early years.

The first not only ran counter to what I thought my professional development should be but also provided what I now think of as the most important broadening and humanizing influence on my first teaching. From my first year at Earlham, like everyone else in the English department, half my teaching time was devoted to the required first-year humanities course. It is not a course to recruit majors, and the genius of its design is that it requires both teacher and student to engage with great works and challenging ideas from many fields. Through that course, I have learned to teach writing and to become more self-conscious about my own writing. I have been able to assign books that I needed to read and think about and to make my own liberal education develop in tandem with my students'. In that course, I have taught *The Prince, The Communist Manifesto, I and Thou, The Dynamics of Faith, Moral Man and Immoral Society*—enormously important texts that I have grappled with in the special way that comes from teaching them. I have also taught Camus, Malraux, Hesse, Trotsky, Tolstoy, Plato, Thomas More, Aristotle, Homer, Aeschylus, and Sophocles. I could identify more than two hundred books—most of them out of my field—that I have taught in that course, which means that they have become a part of the permanent furniture of my mind. Humanities is the course I most enjoy teaching, year in and year out, but only as I have begun to reflect on my own pattern of development as a teacher have I realized how it helped to keep something beyond the specialist alive in me during the early days when the specialist was the easiest side of oneself to develop.

Last spring, I had a chance to talk with a number of alumni who had returned for class reunions. Every significant conversation I had with returning graduates touched in a major way on work that we had done together in the humanities course in 1960, 1965, and 1969. A graduate of five years ago asked whether I remembered our course on utopias and added, "Well, I am still looking for utopia." A graduate of ten years ago thanked me for teaching him to write; another had heard me speak somewhere and teased me for violating a rule that I had laid down in his class in 1965. One person quoted a favorite passage from a book that we had read in 1960. No one apologized or spoke of failure. I do not want to make too much of scanty evidence—I have taught over a thousand students in that humanities class since 1960—but I think I can claim that some of my best development as a teacher parallels some of my best service to students. I believe I can trust the evidence in that lesson.

My second experience that I consider crucial to my development as a teacher is even less orthodox. In spring 1966, a number of students and faculty were talking about ways to develop intensive study programs for the educationally disadvantaged. None of us was sure how it ought to be done, but a handful of senior students asked me to meet with them to work on ways of teaching disadvantaged high school students how to write. About then, the guidelines for the Upward Bound Project were published, and the college decided to apply for Upward Bound funds. The students with whom I had been working asked the academic dean to invite me to become director of the project.

I had already been asked to be a member of the college team at a Danforth Foundation workshop on the liberal arts. This was regarded both as a very important assignment and as a vote of confidence in a junior faculty member. At the workshop, we would work on proposals for reorganizing distribution requirements. It was clear to everyone which way the greater professional advancement lay. At the workshop, I would be identified as a leader in curricular development, work closely with valued colleagues, and meet people from around the country who were doing similar things. But, as a senior colleague said to me, "I think you are making a big mistake, but I knew as soon as the students asked you that you would be so flattered, you would do it."

For the next four summers, I worked with Upward Bound and a prefreshman program that we developed for our own educationally disadvantaged students. In those years, I began to learn something about teaching without the support of grades and credits. I learned the pleasure to be had from helping people who had thought of themselves as losers to get a different picture of themselves. That first summer, we ran something between summer camp and boot camp; we taught, gave first aid, took people on outings, put them to bed at night, and dealt with drunken, abusive parents and suspicious social workers. We followed up the summer with visits to schools and homes, and in a few extraordinary cases, we found ourselves giving support to children who were being taken away from unfit parents or guardians. For the first time, I was sure that my teaching someone to read and write would really help to empower that person. In the next few years, I saw people finishing high school, going on to college, and graduating—breaking free of what had seemed the hopeless trap of poverty. I was gratified to know that, in my role as a teacher of English, I had had something to do with all that.

Working with Upward Bound gave me experience in administering a sizable program, teaching high school students, writing grant proposals, and hiring staff. Other things happened to me as well. I was working with lively, funny, outgoing tenth- and eleventh-graders. They set out to teach me to dance—the Pearl, the Stroll, the Four Corners, the Central State Stomp (all but the last-named looked very much alike to me and my feet)—and they were pleased when I learned anything. Some years later, a close colleage of those years went with a group of faculty and students to an encounter weekend. When I asked him what it had been like, he said, "It was quite interesting, but there wasn't anything there that we hadn't learned in Upward Bound." I think that my four years with Upward Bound opened me up in important ways, most notably by allowing me to feel less diffident about showing affection or receiving affection from colleagues and students. I look back on ways of teaching and ways of being that were immeasurably enriched by my involvement with Upward Bound, especially in that first summer, and then I recall that this event, so important to me in subsequent years, not only had no place in what was conceived of as professional development but was even thought of as a dangerous diversion from the real thing. The plan that emerged from the Danforth conference, by the way, was stillborn.

It is common to speak of teaching as an art. An art is concerned with mastery of a content and development of a craft—both in the sense of the German word *kraft*, which means power, and in the more common sense of clever judgment in presentation of content. Vision is meaningless without the skill to express it or put it into action, but craft is trivial without vision. There must be a dialogic relationship between content and craft, or both are impoverished. Without that interaction, the craftsman is all manner and no substance, and the visionary is a bore.

Teaching as an art involves another dialogue as well, the dialogue between the student and the teacher. The two dialogues overlap as they go on.

The teacher looks continually from the content of the discipline—mathematics or history or chemistry—both to the teacher's craft as mathematician, historian, or chemist and to the student who is trying to learn the discipline. This means that the teacher must practice two crafts, which are by no means alike, the craft of the discipline and the craft of teaching. In the craft of teaching, the teacher must discover how to accommodate the content to the student's comprehension. In the process, it often happens that the teacher is able to enlarge both the student's understanding and the scope of the discipline. I am told, for example, that the periodic table was first developed to help students learn the atomic weight of the elements but that the learning device became a means of predicting elements that were yet to be discovered because it revealed relationships in weight that had not been seen earlier. We have all had the experience, when making something clear to a puzzled student, of achieving new insight into our subject that we might never have gained from traditional research or writing.

In a dialogue, we speak to and are addressed by another. We may ask to be reminded of what we already know, but we also hope to learn what we do not know, to push the limits of our knowledge by our work. As we open ourselves to the subject, the way in which the questions get phrased or the principles are stated is, at least in part, the result of our being addressed by the subject.

When I read *King Lear,* I ask my questions and make my judgments about the action of the play, but if I am fully engaged, I discover that the play is reading me as well. I may start by making judgments about the wisdom of characters' actions, but soon I find the play holding a mirror up to me so that I am forced to evaluate the adequacy of my own life. I come out of the reading changed, purged of emotion, knowing more than I expected. So it can be in any subject. As we set out to teach it, we enter into dialogue with it, and the result can be profound changes in our outlook.

As this dialogue with the subject continues, the dialogue with the student begins. The student may be an apprentice in the discipline or an amateur, a seeker after wisdom or a captive to a required course. In most undergraduate courses, we are likely to have some of each in the class. We talk with out students primarily about the content of the discipline, but that may be only the starting point for the dialogue. We may find that we are required to talk about why the subject is worth studying, why wisdom is worth pursuing, what wisdom is like, why one might devote a lifetime to the subject—all while we are presenting the cognitive material of the discipline.

The dialogue with the student might be proceeding on other levels as well. The student may be confused about values or anxious about relations with other people or undergoing a spiritual crisis, and the questions that result from such issues may not be explicitly stated but operate only to prevent a quick grasp of an assignment or lecture.

All effective teaching—and all effective learning, I believe—is a double dialogue with the discipline and between student and teacher. Even the lecture delivered to a huge hall of anonymous students must be, at the very least, a dialogue with the discipline. The reason why lecturing from yellowed notes signifies deadness is that notes that once represented dialogue now represent only monologue. In the best lectures, the student is stimulated to new ideas by watching the lecturer entertain ideas freshly. The best lectures bring discipline and listener together in the dialogue.

Thinking of teaching as a double dialogue helps me to recognize more clearly what was wrong with my teaching in its early years. I thought that I was introducing students to the systematic study of literature, but I did not realize that the way I was teaching suggested that there was nothing worth doing with my discipline except to write graduate-school papers. I had confused the rigor and integrity of one art — the art of teaching and learning — with the rigor and integrity of another — the discipline of literature. Mine was an innocent confusion — to think that people can treat literature seriously only if they are writing graduate-level papers — but it had damaging effects.

If I understand Erikson, I am enriched by learning how to care, even as I am enriched by being cared for. My development is enhanced both by things which make me feel like an end-in-myself and by things which allow me to be instrumental in the good of others. An important test for our development is the good that it does to others — our students, our colleagues, our families. The alumna whom I described as a prominent social analyst worked with us as a tutor in that first Upward Bound summer, quickly becoming virtually another assistant director, working closely with us to handle the most complex problems. She has since said that the experience of working in that program with such broad responsibility gave her confidence, for the first time, that she had significant skills. She dates the initiatives that have made her a prominent writer to that time.

What Erikson says about us as the teaching species has profound implications for curricular, institutional, professional, and personal development. To enhance teaching means working on its social qualities, working on the milieu in which teaching occurs, encouraging teachers to reflect not only on subject matter and mode of delivery but also on the teacher's relation to learners and the quality of caring expressed in the teaching. It means examining the traditional professional activities of research and writing for their contribution to the psychosocial development of the individual or their impact on the teaching milieu, rather than assuming that any research makes for personal refreshment and better teaching. It means considering professional and institutional needs in the context of what research in human development tells us our students need. Emphatically, it also means examining the institution to see that it does not overvalue the teacher as technician and undervalue the person who teaches.

Artists learn a craft for which they have aptitudes, but they have to work at the craft, in part through imitation and apprenticeship, and their vision comes in and through the craft that they practice. Moreover, artists learn by watching each other work and by seeing the end products of that work. In contrast, in most colleges, the classroom door is tightly closed. No one comes in without an invitation — which means in practice that no one comes in — and what a teacher does is a secret between the teacher and the class. What are we likely to learn from one another under such circumstances? We know only what the student grapevine says or what the individual teacher says about how a given class is going. Typically, we do not talk about our classes except when we have had either a very bad or a very good day. This hardly constitutes dependable evidence on which to build an understanding of teaching.

The first step toward better insight into our teaching is to legitimize conversation about the craft of teaching, and that means giving ourselves something concrete to talk about. What are my goals in a discussion? Do different disciplines have different goals? Do my students agree on goals for discussion? What am I looking for in assigning a term paper? How do I describe the assignment in order to get best results? What do I want to achieve with the comments I put on the paper? What do I want the student to do with those comments? How do I think the student will learn from my comments? Do I conceive of them as the final word on the paper or as the continuation of a conversation?

Some of the best work that I have done in the past year, I believe, results from asking the colleagues who invite me to consult with them on their teaching to identify their greatest strengths, what in themselves they respect most, and then to determine how they can use those strengths for the benefit of the course and the needs of the students.

That is, I have tried to get completely away from the issue of correcting weaknesses. Instead, I ask colleagues, "What are your strengths, and how can they best be used to serve your students and your goals as a teacher?" In talking with several graduating seniors, I found myself asking them to reflect on their college careers in some way. I asked, "If I were to write a letter of reference for you that described the strengths you have and value most, what would they be?"

Both kinds of conversation have been moving. Neither my colleagues nor my students talked easily about strengths at first. We have all been trained to feel better about confessing faults than about acknowledging strengths that we respect in ourselves. When student and colleagues do start to talk about them, I notice that they value the strengths of being over those of doing. They want to be respected for qualities of their relationships to others, if they have to choose, not for knowing the material perfectly. But, of course, what they want — what we want — is the right balance between head and heart. That is, the caring and nurturing qualities, the effective serving of others and of principle, are the strengths our colleagues and students value most highly, just as we do. These qualities seem to be at the center of the craft of teaching. I suggest that they are also an appropriate starting point for faculty development activities.

Reference

Erikson, E. *Insight and Responsibility.* New York: Norton, 1964.

Paul A. Lacey is Bain-Swiggett Professor of English at Earlham College, director of the Lilly Endowment's Postdoctoral Teaching Awards Program for 1980–82, and author of The Inner War *(Philadelphia: Fortress Press, 1972), a study of five contemporary American poets.*

A fascinating look at the way in which a young teacher regards her work with students.

Self-Evaluation and Prospectus

Linda Clader

In order to evaluate my teaching, I must first try to explain my goals. I find that this is not a simple exercise, for my goals have changed over the years, and I expect that they will continue to change as I continue to think about them. If the following statement looks a bit blurred, I hope that it is the result of the motion, not of the fog.

The goals can be defined by means of a threefold question: Why teach, how to teach, and why teach the classics? The longer I engage in this profession, the more clearly I realize that I enjoy teaching because I like people, especially because I like watching and helping them grow. Certainly, I do not limit this enjoyment to the classroom, for I get the same boost from working with colleagues and even with "civilians." But it is the involvement with the growth of another individual that excites me—and terrifies me—about the vocation that I have chosen to follow.

Like a second-level student in William Perry's scheme of intellectual and ethical development, I used to assume that one could help another only if one felt that one held the truth, and that only didactic or exemplary means were needed to impart it. This idealistic—as well as simplistic—view of teaching presented problems, for I was well aware

Written at the request of the Tenure Review Committee at Carleton College.

at the outset of my career that I had only a glimmer of some truth, and that I would have to work forever to attain the elevated status of wise woman. After several years of teaching, however, and having reached perhaps the fifth stage of Perry's nine stages in my prolonged adolescence, I realized that I never would hold the truth, that my perception would always differ from that of any other individual, and that, in any case, the teacher's job was to help a student develop his or her own views, illuminated and challenged but not dictated by the views of others. What a simple but liberating discovery: My job was to learn to ask the right questions, not to supply the right answer.

This assumption about teaching applies to all aspects of my work at Carleton, and it helps me to define the style in which I take on my various tasks. Clearly, my most structured contacts with students are in the classroom, within the context of my discipline, and they emphasize intellectual over ethical, spiritual, or personal development. But I have no difficulty considering that aspect of my teaching as just one of many types of contacts, and accordingly, I take my roles as adviser, fellow committee-member, and soprano or crumhorner as seriously as I do the role of classroom teacher. In all these contacts, the same theory applies: A person is a composite of many different, recognizable, interconnected components; as a result, it is impossible to isolate one part and forget all the others. Our major task as teachers is to develop the intellectual potential of our students, but just as we cannot entirely divorce our own heads from our hearts, neither can we exclude all consideration of nonintellectual areas in our students' lives. Perhaps I enjoy working with Pro Musica so much because it gives me a chance to deal more directly with these other sides of students — and myself. In that setting, I am a student, too, although I am frequently given more organizational responsibility than the younger members, and we work together on breathing, tuning our stubborn instruments (a throat, in my case), and managing to stay friendly as a concert approaches. The experience provides marvelous therapy for me, and I believe that the students enjoy working on the same level with a person who may one day have to grade their papers. In these situations, as in committee work, I assume that one of my functions is to model how an educated but eminently vulnerable and fallible human being behaves in society. I have no illusions that I always live up to the standards that I envision, but I figure that, at the very least, I can show them how it looks to give it a whirl.

My teaching style, then, is to be a model, to present to the students an example of the classicist or humanist at work, and even to let them in a bit on how a classicist or humanist deals with life in general. Because I am so interested in the students' (and my own) growth as whole persons, I feel obligated to show them myself as a person — up to a point, at least—so the style I have adopted also implies openness and vulnerability. Some students react negatively to this approach, but most seem to find it reassuring. All I know is that I am comfortable with it: It allows me not only to present material that I feel confident about and to gush with delight at those aspects of the classics that I especially love but also to try out ideas that lie at the edges of my competence—and still believe that I am teaching something important. It also allows me to explore my feelings about literature and life and thus, I think, to encourage my students to do the same.

The preceding paragraphs are supposed to answer the questions "Why teach?" and "How to teach?" The third question, "Why teach the classics?" should be simpler to answer now, for this particular medium for teaching fits well with the approach that I am developing. Clearly, literature is about life, and the greatest literature is about growth of one kind or another. On one level, I enjoy the opportunity to be the first to help students to encounter Achilles, Odysseus, Aeneas, or Oedipus (the heroic figures of myth all illustrate aspects of living that students can identify with); on another level, I enjoy helping them learn to communicate with a dead poet from a dead civilization (the exercise broadens their understanding of people in general by forcing them to listen to what the artist is really saying and to take into account the context within which he is saying it); on still another level, I enjoy helping a group to make these discoveries for themselves through the medium of class discussion (classical literature is, of course, eternally discussable). I knew long ago that I wanted to teach, but only much later did I decide what my medium was to be. Now I feel a strong commitment to the classics for all the reasons I have just mentioned, but it is easy to see that these reasons are primarily instructional. There is another, more personal aspect to my commitment, of course. How else could I get paid to read Homer several times a year? That quiet joy remains unmentioned in polite conversation.

As I reread what I have just written, it strikes me as sounding a bit idealistic. So now for the facts of the case. The approach to teaching that I have chosen contains inherent drawbacks. The great danger in considering all of my activity with students as part of my teaching is that I can become totally wrapped up in the college; I believe that this danger may be particularly acute for an unmarried person, for a good part of my time is spent with students and in campus activities. Moreover, as my life becomes more and more identified with my broadly defined profession, it is easier to see myself primarily as a teacher, to evaluate my worth as a person in terms of my success as an educator—that is, when classes go well, everything is beautiful; when they go poorly, all is rotten. So the theory about teaching to which I now hold involves some risk, and as long as I remain committed to this theory, I must beware of its pitfalls and entanglements. Indeed, there have been times when I wondered how I could survive the year and whether I had the emotional strength to cope with the profession. So to stick to this approach to teaching necessarily implies accepting a certain amount of instability in my existence.

More narrowly, my goals and teaching techniques frequently do not match well. Although I love to watch students grapple with a question themselves, I also love to bestow my own brilliant insights upon them. The danger lies in doing too much expounding and too little listening. I want them to watch an analytical mind at work in order to have it as a model, but I also want them to attempt the same operation. When I let go and lecture, the students stop speaking; when I hold back and listen, my manner can become so low-key that I fear they will fall asleep. This problem arises most frequently in small classes, where the major activity is translating a work; in large survey courses, I happily continue to lecture in a style comfortable to me—lots of spiels by teacher with as much student participation as teacher can evoke.

More broadly, I feel capable of pursuing the goals that I have adopted only when all is right with my world. I am aware that I have gained a reputation in this institution for being strong and positive; nevertheless, inside me there is a shy and hypersensitive creature who sometimes finds it an enormous challenge just to make it through a day with students. On the bad days, it is easy to retreat into that comfortable bastion inhabited by so many classicists—the authority of the texts. Secondary material does not matter: What does Aeschylus say? What kind of subjunctive is Vergil using and why? Another word for such retreat is laziness, but I have long been convinced that laziness does not really exist in itself; rather, it signals fear of something. This paragraph seems to meander, but I have never tried to write any of this down before, and my thoughts are not all lined up. I suppose that the point is, when I feel fearful—of allowing myself to appear vulnerable to students or colleagues, of feeling incompetent in my field, about a matter pertaining to my future, or about a situation in my private life—I sometimes do not teach in harmony with the goals that I have espoused.

The press of time is another impediment to success in teaching as I want to teach. Although I enjoy committee work and see it as a legitimate aspect of my work as a teacher, I often feel that the balance between that activity and my other commitments does not accurately reflect their relative importance. More than the actual number of hours required by committee work, I find that the drain on my psychic energy is the most insidious block placed on my teaching by the governance system. Perhaps I am endowed with limited creativity, but I know that when I am heavily involved in a collegewide issue, my preparation for courses suffers. The conflict came home to me most vividly a few years ago during the presidential search, at which time I discovered that, although I was spending a good number of hours every week doing work directly related to the search, the problems of that activity so dominated my thoughts that I was, in effect, carrying committee work about all the time and that I had little energy to spare for the more mundane affairs of the college—like my classes. I recognize that that year was unusual. Nevertheless, in a smaller or less focused way, all campus activities compete with the classroom, and because I enjoy both kinds of work, the conflict is a major problem for me. I have a strong commitment to this institution, and I believe that I can and should serve the institution in several capacities, but I become frustrated when service to the community detracts from what I perceive to be my primary function. Certainly, this problem is not peculiar to me, but it is real enough.

In a nutshell, although the rambling account of my theory of teaching may make the activity sound like unmitigated bliss, I find that teaching is difficult and that it demands a great deal of energy and constant awareness. Perhaps it will become easier with the years. In any case, if it did not present a challenge, it would not be nearly so much fun.

It is always easier to speak of the negatives about oneself than of the positives, and one draft of this opus entirely omitted the positive stuff on the assumption that it was all implicit in the goals. Then I decided that perhaps only I would be able to read in the implications, so here begins the horn-tooting (crumhorn, mind you). At the lowest level, I think I know something about my field. I used to be afraid that I would be discovered for the ignoramus that I knew I was, although they never discovered this truth at Harvard, where I knew that I was the only mistake the Department of Classics had made on admissions; but after teaching some of this material a few times now, I feel comfortable enough about what I do know to be comfortable admitting to what I do not. I think I reached that plateau after teaching Greek 2 twice— I actually believe that I have conquered the Greek verb, an achievement roughly equivalent to climbing Mt. Everest, especially as perceived by a Greek 2 student. Teaching Greek and Latin literature in translation is a great aid to increased confidence, too, for those courses require such wide reading in such a short amount of time that either you learn everything there is to know about the classics in ten weeks or you learn to cope with not knowing it. Somehow, I have come to the point where I see the great unknown as a challenge, not a threat; this makes learning that much more delicious.

My colleague tells me that I am also good at creating an atmosphere in which students feel that they can try out their ideas without being put down. I was happy to be told that, for I consciously strive toward that goal, and as a result, I worry when a student suggests that he or she has felt that I was sarcastic or caustic in class. No one has sat in on any of my advising sessions, but I believe that my advisees (official or not) also feel comfortable in one-to-one situations. Certainly, my own comfort in a teaching context influences that of the students, and I have been delighted to discover that as I grow older my comfort increases. Oddly, perhaps, it seems that as the gap in age between the students and me increases, I feel more ready to take risks, to express ignorance, or to be assertive in making recommendations. It is pleasing to be able to identify areas of growth in oneself! More specifically, I am particularly proud of the fact that I can elicit discussion from large classes. (Whew! I don't think I can stand any more of this.) I am also an adequate soprano and an accomplished sight reader.

My instructional goals, at this point, consist largely of becoming more comfortable with myself in order to better encounter the students and of becoming more informed about the kinds of problems with which they must deal on both intellectual and personal levels. William Perry's book, *Forms of Intellectual and Ethical Development,* was an enormous help in envisioning these goals. My academic goals are to become more familiar with the classical corpus (I would love someday to be able to quote vast passages of Greek and Latin — to myself, of course) and with English and European literature. There is a twofold reason for the latter. European literature, as it derives from the Latin, can be illuminating to students who are struggling with the derivative nature of the Latin literature itself. Speaking more personally, I feel like an illiterate when I find myself in the company of old-time classicists, who seem to derive such joy from the English poets. For this reason, too, I hope to become an educated person. More specifically, I am becoming interested in the development of genre, and I hope to pursue my interest in several literatures. My latest passion is classical pastoral — I love what Vergil does with the form, and I am fascinated by Pope's adaptations of the ancient tradition. At the moment, I expect to focus my work during sabbatical on that area, although I have no particular end in mind.

I have a more institutional goal as well. I have become interested and active in the area of faculty development, and I have come to the realization that part of the reason for my interest is identical with my reason for teaching — watching and helping people to grow. If I did not believe that teaching is asking questions rather than providing answers, my desire to continue in this area would be pure hybris. But I think that I can do more work with faculty on the improvement of teaching without pretending to be a master teacher myself, and I hope that I shall have the opportunity to do so. This is an exciting aspect of what a college is about and a most rewarding activity for me.

In summary, I believe that I have grown considerably from the timid graduate student who arrived here in 1972, and the confidence and excitement that I now feel encourage me to anticipate the future with relish rather than terror. I could date my breakthrough to the time of my third-year review, when a combination of reassurance from my superiors and new awareness of what I was doing (brought about primarily by my work on the Teaching Methods Committee, the first summer institute, and the Old Teaching Methods Seminar) gave me the first real boost in confidence that I needed to begin feeling like an adult. I still feel frightened, depressed, and inadequate at times, but for the most part I am happy about the process in which I am engaged.

Let me close with one final comment on the preceding. I have agonized, grumbled, and procrastinated about this exercise, but I must also admit that I have found it to be enormously useful. My annual reports have occasionally provided an excuse for some soul-searching and thundering, but never before have I felt compelled to try something as comprehensive as this essay. I wonder: If we were all invited to engage in activities of this sort, and often, would we become a stronger academic community?

References

Perry, W. G., Jr. *Forms of Intellectual and Ethical Development.* New York: Holt, Rinehart and Winston, 1968.

A Homerist, Linda Clader is an associate professor of classical languages at Carleton College, and chairman of the department. Her major scholarly interest is now Latin poetry.

A seasoned professional in faculty development discusses
some of the most useful resources in this area.

Strategies Galore:
Resources for
Faculty Development

Robert E. Young

A good place to start one's reading is the reports of the Project to Improve College Teaching, cosponsored ty the American Association of University Professors and the American Association of Colleges. The project is well summarized in:

Eble, K. *Professors as Teachers.* San Francisco: Jossey-Bass, 1972.

Next, read this widely discussed pamphlet:

The Group for Human Development in Higher Education. *Faculty Development in a Time of Retrenchment.* New Rochelle, N.Y.: Change Publications, 1974.

This publication provided much of the inspiration for early thinking and work in the field. It also responded to the first wave of concern over "lack of mobility" and "professional stagnation." Its strategy was to put the professional development of college teachers at the center of institutional discussions. George Bonham, the editor of *Change,* wrote in the preface: "One cannot help but feel that one or two dozen copies, strategically distributed to the men and women who ordinarily make things happen on campus, might develop change strategies that may surprise even veteran cynics." He was right.

The "movement" by then was underway, but many programs resembled a simple collection of activities and were not well informed by an understanding of human development, pedagogy, or institutions. What was needed was a conceptual framework to guide the development of more comprehensive strategies. Eventually, two works appeared that partly filled this need:

Bergquist, W. H., and Phillips, S. R. "Components of an Effective Faculty Development Program." *Journal of Higher Education,* 1975, *46,* 177–211.
Bergquist, W. H., and Phillips, S. R. *A Handbook for Faculty Development.* Washington, D.C.: Council for the Advancement of Small Colleges, 1975.

These works reflected the experiences of an early core of individuals involved in professional development programs. These publications gave the field an idea that has defined it as much as any other: significant change, especially in professional competence, depends on a person's attitude toward the work, the processes used to pursue it, and the structure in which the work is done. Effective faculty development programs need to address all three. To each, Bergquist and Phillips attached a label. Activities to influence attitude became *professional development,* process was the concern of *instructional development,* and working with structure was referred to as *organization development.* These labels continue to be used by people writing and working in faculty development. Since the first *Handbook,* a second has appeared, and a third is now in preparation. All are available through the Council for the Advancement of Small Colleges (CASC).

Scores of campuses took up professional development in the middle 1970s, and the group of educators working full-time in the area began to increase. Strategies proliferated to the point where two administrators interested in professional development could put together an article like:

Brown, D. G., and Hanger, S. "130 Pieces of a Faculty Development Program." *Educational Record,* 1975, *56,* 201–206.

Jerry Gaff performed an important national study of faculty development:

Gaff, J. *Toward Faculty Renewal.* San Francisco: Jossey-Bass, 1975.

This book, widely respected in the field, includes sections on organization, politics, financing, staffing, impact, and prospects for the future of faculty development.

A good look at the strategies employed by some of the sixteen colleges involved in a project sponsored by the Society for Values in Higher Education is provided in a later book edited by Gaff:

Gaff, J. (Ed.). *New Directions for Higher Education: Institutional Renewal Through the Improvement of Teaching,* no. 24. San Francisco: Jossey-Bass, 1978.

From the beginning, a strong theme in the work has been the personal and social development of college faculty and administrators. Those who have been thinking along this line emphasize the need to pursue new roles, not just for professional development but for more general human development. They propose a "new way of thinking about faculty development as involving not simply greater professional competence but heightened self-awareness and broadened perspective on the world" (Freedman, 1973, p. v). Nevitt Sanford, Mervin Freedman, and their colleagues at the Wright Institute and elsewhere have studied the development of faculty and administrators within the culture of colleges and universities and written thoughtfully about their findings in numerous publications, including:

Freedman, M. (Ed.). *New Directions for Higher Education: Facilitating Faculty Development,* no. 1. San Francisco: Jossey-Bass, 1973.
Freedman, M., and others. *Academic Culture and Faculty Development.* Berkeley, Calif.: Montaigne Press, 1979.
Sanford, N. *Learning After College.* Berkeley, Calif.: Montaigne Press, 1980.

Another contribution to the practice of professional development has been the approach of the National Training Laboratory (NTL). A number of people who were trained at NTL and involved with its programs took an early interest in faculty development. Their work focused on group functioning and organization climate as important factors in professional growth. The use of campus "change teams" to pursue development has been a frequently used strategy. The following provide good examples of this approach.

Sikes, W., Schlesinger, L., and Seashore, C. *Renewing Higher Education from Within: A Guide for Campus Change Teams.* San Francisco: Jossey-Bass, 1974.
Sikes, W., and Barrett, L. *Case Studies on Faculty Development.* Washington, D.C.: Council for the Advancement of Small Colleges, 1976.

As approaches to faculty development proliferated, a second, related "movement" was underway: faculty evaluation. Faculty had always been evaluated, even by students, but the influence of a general concern for accountability in American society and a parallel interest in professional development put strategies for faculty evaluation on center stage during the 1970s. For an overview of where things were and where they now are in this area, read:

Miller, R. *Developing Programs for Faculty Evaluation: A Sourcebook for Higher Education.* San Francisco: Jossey-Bass, 1974.
O'Connell, W. R., and Smartt, S. H. *Improving Faculty Evaluation: A Trial in Strategy.* Atlanta: Southern Regional Education Board, 1979.

One book in particular has pulled together much of the theory and practice of professional development. Everyone interested in this area should read:

Lindquist, J. (Ed.). *Designing Teaching Improvement Programs.* Berkeley, Calif.: Pacific Soundings Press, 1978. (Now available from the Council for the Advancement of Small Colleges.)

Its special feature is chapters on professional development in different types of settings—liberal arts college, university, community college, nontraditional college, and consortium of colleges. Another book by Lindquist deserves serious study for the extensive use it makes of case studies:

Lindquist, J. *Strategies for Change: Innovations as Adaptive Development.* Berkeley, Calif.: Pacific Soundings Press, 1978. (Now available from the Council for the Advancement of Small Colleges.)

A concern for program evaluation began to develop late in the decade. Here is a short list of readings in the evaluation methodologies area:

Centra, J. A. *Faculty Development Practices in U.S. Colleges and Universities.* Princeton, N.J.: Educational Testing Service, 1976.
Davis, J. A. *Instructional Improvement—An Assessment of Programs at Sixteen Universities.* Pullman, Wash.: Information Futures, 1978.
Hoyt, D. P., and Howard, G. S. "The Evaluation of Faculty Development Programs." *Research in Higher Education,* 1978, *8,* 25-38.
McMillan, J. H. "The Unfinished Business of Evaluation in Faculty Development." Occasional Paper No. 13. Evanston, Ill.: Center for the Teaching Professionals, Northwestern University, 1977.

Nelson, W. C., and Siegel, M. E. *Effective Approaches to Faculty Development.* Washington, D.C.: American Associaton of Colleges, 1979.
O'Connell, W. R., and Meeth, L. R. *Evaluating Teaching Improvement Programs.* New Rochelle, N.Y.: Change Publications, 1978.
Stakenas, R., Mayo, G. D., and Peterson, G. *Faculty Development and Evaluations: A Look at Its Present Status in the Southern Region.* Atlanta: Undergraduate Education Reform Project, Southern Regional Education Board, 1979.
Wergin, J. F. "Evaluating Faculty Development Programs." In J. A. Centra (Ed.), *New Directions for Higher Education: Renewing and Evaluating Teaching,* no. 17. San Francisco: Jossey-Bass, 1977.

In the last few years, professional development programs have expanded to embrace administrative development as well. Useful publications include:

American Council on Education. *A Guide to Professional Development Opportunities for College and University Administrators.* Washington, D.C.: American Council on Education (published annually).
Fischer, C. "The Evaluation and Development of College and University Administrators." *Research Currents,* March 1977, pp. 3–6.
Nordvall, R. C. *Evaluation and Development of Adminstrators.* Washington, D.C.: American Association for Higher Education, 1979.
Shtogren, J. A. (Ed.). *Administrative Development in Higher Education: State of the Art.* Richmond, Va.: Higher Education Leadership and Management Society, 1978.

In the future, professional development may come to address broader issues related to career planning, issues raised in:

American Association for Higher Education. *Faculty Career Development.* Washington, D.C.: American Association for Higher Education, 1977.

Recently, interest in the nature of work and careers has increased both inside and outside higher education, and there is a growing sense that the adult development research of people like Daniel Levinson should be taken more seriously by faculty and administrators. As the population as a whole takes a closer look at the quality of work life, some of this will undoubtedly rub off onto faculty.

Where would I go? I would go to conferences, workshops, and seminars, and I would visit existing programs; or better yet, if I were planning a program or a new approach to an ongoing program, I would send one or two faculty or staff members for whom the program is being planned. The research on change shows that new ideas brought back by group members often result in successful innovations. The *Chronicle of Higher Education* is the best place to identify future events.

Beyond one-shot programs each year, a number of universities and organizations sponsor seminars and workshops related to faculty development in higher education. Among the longest standing are the University of Michigan and the Cornell summer courses, the Sagamore Seminar by the Center for Instructional Development at Syracuse University, the NTL Summer Workshops, the AAC Summer Deans Institute, and the Harvard Educational Management Seminar. Also, each year major conferences deal with faculty and administrative development, either exclusively or as an important part of a larger program. A quick list would include:

> American Association for Higher Education (AAHE) conferences in the early 1970s stimulated much of the work in faculty development. It continues to be the place to hear about "what's new."

> Professional and Organizational Development Network Annual Conference. (This organization has become a major point of identification for people involved in professional development and a clearinghouse for information.)

> (Also, the National Council for Staff, Program, and Organizational Development, the Association for Education Communication and Technology, Division of Instructional Development, and the American Education Research Association-Special Interest Group of Faculty and Instructional Development have conferences each year.)

> American Association of University Administrators Annual Conference.

> Faculty Development and Evaluation in Higher Education (early spring since 1977, sponsored by the Institute for Higher Education, University of Florida.

> International Conference on Improving University Teaching (University College, University of Maryland). Each summer since 1975.

How would I keep up? The concepts and realities of faculty development will change as society and higher education change, and as programs for faculty influence what we mean by professional development. Let me suggest a few ways to keep up with the thinking and activity in this area.

First, the professional organizations whose conferences I mentioned earlier each represent a group of people interested and involved in professional development. If I could choose only one, I think it would be POD, because it has links to each of the others. Next, the journals provide a way of keeping up. I suggest a regular review of *Chronicle, Change, Improving College and University Teaching,* and *Journal of Higher Education.* I would also subscribe to *Faculty Development and Evaluation in Higher Education: A Quarterly Newspaper* (edited by Al Smith at the Institute for Higher Education, University of Florida). Finally, a good way to take a regular look at examples of other approaches is to get on the mailing list of campus programs that publish newsletters. Organizations like POD and AERA's Special Interest Group on Faculty and Instructional Development know which programs have useful publications. Most of these are free of charge.

An inexpensive introduction to the resources in the area is:

Gaff, S. S., and others. *Professional Development: A Guide to Resources.* New Rochelle, N.Y.: Change Magazine Press, 1978.

This brief guide to resources for planning and evaluating professional development programs can be very useful in stimulating your thinking or in actually helping you implement a program. But don't forget another most accessible resource: the faculty and staff or your own campus. As professionals, faculty members and administrators have insights — sometimes hard-won and intently held — into their own development and that of their colleagues that will never surface in the literature or at conferences on faculty and administrative development. They — along with you — can know what will work at your institution, in your school, or in your department, in ways that the authors and presenters of professional development cannot know.

Before becoming director of institutional development at the University of North Dakota, Robert E. Young was associate director of the Center for Improving Teaching Effectiveness at Virginia Commonwealth University. He is guest editor of New Directions for Teaching and Learning: Fostering Critical Thinking, *no. 3, 1980 (Jossey-Bass Publishers).*

Paying more attention to our teaching
is a good way to continue learning.

Deliberate Teaching

John F. Noonan

Our teaching can become an even richer experience for students and four us as well if we reflect on it more purposefully. This belief in the value of deliberation unites the chapters in this volume, although the individual contexts differ. Writing letters to students is quite different from analyzing former favorite teachers, yet in an important way, both Richard Jones and Thomas McGovern testify to the worth of mulling over our work with students. So does Linda Clader, who, by paying attention to her assumptions about teaching, invites us to consider our own presuppositions and to share them openly with others.

The belief in open discourse about teaching is a second strand that links these chapters. Peter Elbow's methods for visiting colleagues' classes require little more than the willingness to express responses to their teaching always as personal reactions, not as "objective" assessments. Such commentary is valuable precisely because it is the view of one person, a point about criticism sometimes overlooked by those who write about evaluation. Paul Lacey's meditation on two decades spent in the classroom has a similar autobiographical edge to it, which is why reading it makes us more sensitive to the patterns of our own careers. Perhaps this is what the photographer Diane Arbus meant when she said that the more specific a thing is, the more general it is.

What could be more singular than Emily Hancock's meeting with the teaching assistant, or Annette Woodlief's experience teaching the course on women writers, or Judith Newcombe's transition to stu-

98

dent-centeredness? Reading these essays reminds us that growth does not occur in linear fashion, that the specific moments of our work with students have a volume which, when explored with care, can make us more discerning. When we see a course as composed of countless separate moments, we allow ourselves to be stimulated by those moments.

Once in a while, a faculty member will stop by my office and say something like, "The trouble with teaching is that it is not rewarded." That may always be true in some settings; it is also true that, in any setting, teaching is not always rewarding. Sometimes, we seem to be getting little back for our efforts, and our batteries run down. While the causes of this drainage are complex, reading the chapters in this book leads me to think that there may be steps that we can take to improve the exchange: We can stop now and then and consider what we are learning—about the discipline, about students, about teaching, about learning, about ourselves. These authors tell us that when we include ourselves in our courses and view them more deliberately, our courses become more rewarding.

John F. Noonan is the director of the Center for Improving Teaching Effectiveness at Virgina Commonwealth University and coeditor-in-chief (with Kenneth Eble) of this series, New Directions for Teaching and Learning.

Index

New Directions Quarterly Sourcebooks

New Directions for Teaching and Learning is one of several distinct series of quarterly sourcebooks published by Jossey-Bass. The sourcebooks in each series are designed to serve both as *convenient compendiums* of the latest knowledge and practical experience on their topics and as *long-life reference tools.*

One-year, four-sourcebook subscriptions for each series cost $18 for individuals (when paid by personal check) and $30 for institutions, libraries, and agencies. Single copies of earlier sourcebooks are available at $6.95 each *prepaid* (or $7.95 each when *billed*).

A complete listing is given below of current and past sourcebooks in the *New Directions for Teaching and Learning* series. The titles and editors-in-chief of the other series are also listed. To subscribe, or to receive further information, write: New Directions Subscriptions, Jossey-Bass Inc., Publishers, 433 California Street, San Francisco, California 94104.

New Directions for Teaching and Learning
Kenneth E. Eble and John F. Noonan, Editors-in-Chief
1980: 1. *Improving Teaching Styles,* Kenneth E. Eble
       2. *Learning, Cognition, and College Teaching,*
         Wilbert J. McKeachie
       3. *Fostering Critical Thinking,* Robert E. Young

New Directions for Child Development
William Damon, Editor-in-Chief

New Directions for College Learning Assistance
Kurt V. Lauridsen, Editor-in-Chief

New Directions for Community Colleges
Arthur M. Cohen, Editor-in-Chief
Florence B. Brawer, Associate Editor

New Directions for Continuing Education
Alan B. Knox, Editor-in-Chief

New Directions for Exceptional Children
James J. Gallagher, Editor-in-Chief

New Directions for Experiential Learning
Pamela J. Tate, Editor-in-Chief
Morris T. Keeton, Consulting Edito